THE FUTURE OF DISABILITY LAW

THE FUTURE OF DISABILITY LAW

ESSAYS FROM THE 2015 JACOBUS TENBROEK DISABILITY LAW SYMPOSIUM

Edited by

DAVID FERLEGER, ESQ.

THE FUTURE OF DISABILITY LAW
Essays from the 2015 Jacobus tenBroek Disability Law Symposium

Cover photo: Dr. Jacobus tenBroek (1911–1968), founder and president of the National Federation of the Blind.

iUniverse books may be ordered through booksellers or by contacting:

iUniverse
1663 Liberty Drive
Bloomington, IN 47403
www.iuniverse.com
1-800-Authors (1-800-288-4677)

Because of the dynamic nature of the Internet, any web addresses or links contained in this book may have changed since publication and may no longer be valid. The views expressed in this work are solely those of the author and do not necessarily reflect the views of the publisher, and the publisher hereby disclaims any responsibility for them.

Any people depicted in stock imagery provided by Thinkstock are models, and such images are being used for illustrative purposes only. Certain stock imagery © Thinkstock.

ISBN: 978-1-4917-8358-0 (sc)
ISBN: 978-1-4917-8359-7 (e)

Print information available on the last page.

iUniverse rev. date: 02/24/2016

Table of Contents

Shaping Culture Change

Shaping the Judiciary

Shaping the Issues

Preface

It has been an honor to edit and prepare this volume for the National Federation of the Blind (NFB). The NFB is the largest organization of blind and low-vision people in the United States. Founded in 1940, the Federation has grown to over fifty-thousand members. The organization consists of affiliates and local chapters in every state, the District of Columbia, and Puerto Rico.

The founder and president of the National Federation of the Blind for its first twenty years was Dr. Jacobus tenBroek, a professor, lawyer, and constitutional scholar. He led early battles to obtain a modest stipend for blind people so they could live independently (security), have equal access to jobs in the Civil Service and elsewhere where blind candidates had been prohibited from applying (opportunity), and enjoy equal access to housing, transportation, and places of public accommodation (equality).

The foresight of Dr. Marc Maurer, immediate past president of the NFB, established the annual Jacobus tenBroek Disability Law Symposium some years ago. Mark Riccobono, current NFB President, facilitated the transformation of the 2015 symposium into this book. Unique among many works in the field, this volume presents the scholarship, opinions, and experiences of scholars, advocates, and people with disabilities who come together on an equal footing.

Lou Ann Blake at the NFB makes the tenBroek symposia possible by her astute leadership and plain hard work. She supported this book to its completion as well.

In addition to my deep appreciation to Dr. Marc Maurer, President Mark Riccobono, and Ms. Lou Ann Blake, I thank Sofia Tamimi, who is beginning her legal career, for her thoughtful and careful editorial assistance.

David Ferleger
Editor

Introduction:
Pathways to Disabilities Justice

David Ferleger[1]

The prophet Amos said to the king: "I am no prophet. Neither am I a prophet's son. But I am a herdsman and a grower of sycamore figs."[2] I am not a grower of figs, but like the other authors in this book, I am aware of the difficulty in prophesying.

Envisioning the future is essential to shaping the future. This volume looks to the past and present as the threshold to a more just world for all people, including people with disabilities. The prophet Amos shared that stance. Amos believed in social justice; he is the source of the famous line by Dr. Martin Luther King, Jr. in the "I Have a Dream" speech: "No, no, we are not satisfied and will not be satisfied until justice rolls down like water and righteousness like a mighty stream."[3]

Consider some of our own history. When he was carried in a sedan chair to the constitutional convention, Benjamin Franklin could not have predicted that eventually there would be Segways and motorized wheelchairs. Governor Morris, who helped draft the Constitution and became a senator for New York, wore what they called a rough stick to

---

[1] David Ferleger, editor of this volume, is a "Philadelphia lawyer," and author, and he has a national consulting and litigation practice, including before the Supreme Court of the United States. He has been appointed by federal courts as a special master, a court-appointed monitor, and a technical advisor in several disability justice lawsuits. http://www.ferleger.com.

[2] Amos 7:14.

[3] Amos 5:24. Dr. Martin Luther King, Jr., "I Have a Dream." Delivered August 28, 1963, at the Lincoln Memorial, Washington, DC.

replace the left leg that he lost in a carriage accident in 1790. He would not have been able to predict today's prosthetics.

There are other things that are hard to predict. In the 1800s, many states enacted the "ugly laws," forbidding people with disabilities from being on the street.[4] That sounds pretty strange and old, but these ugly laws were not repealed in many places until the 1970s, the last one in Chicago in 1974.

What does the future hold? I see the possibility for a number of future pathways for what I call "disability justice."[5] These are not posed as alternatives. These may develop simultaneously. Perhaps each pathway may be considered as backup to the others, thus multiplying the likelihood of overall progress.

One pathway involves renewed attention to rights under the United States Constitution. Current litigation often ignores the Constitution. After all, some think, we have the Americans with Disabilities Act, the Rehabilitation Act, the right to education and other statutes. Of what assistance would constitutional rights be? I believe that it is possible, as the Supreme Court changes, which it will, that there will be a constitutional prohibition of discrimination against people with disabilities. It may be circumscribed in some ways, but I believe there will be room under the Constitution for recognition of disability justice claims. I wrote a law review article advocating this result several years ago.[6] Especially for people, (and perhaps initially only for people) confined in institutions, I think there's an argument under the Constitution to prohibit the use of congregate institutions. The *Olmstead v. L.C. by Zimring*, 527 U.S.

---

[4] For example, Chicago's Ugly Law stated:
No person who is diseased, maimed, mutilated or in any way deformed so as to be an unsightly or disgusting object or improper person to be allowed in or on the public ways or other public places in this city, or shall therein or thereon expose himself to public view, under a penalty of not less than one dollar nor more than fifty dollars for each offense.
City of Chicago Municipal Code, sec. 36034 (1881)

[5] I prefer "disability justice" over what I consider to be the narrower "disability rights." Disability justice encompasses rights but also encompasses broad fairness notions, which evolve with social and cultural change.

[6] *See* Ferleger, *The Constitutional Right to Community Services*, 26 Ga. St. U.L. Rev. 763 (2010).

581 (1999) case addressed discrimination under the Americans with Disabilities Act and carefully avoided the constitutional question. That question remains open.[7] A constitutional right would be much harder to constrict or amend than a statute.

Another pathway would be that the United States adopt the international Convention on the Rights of People with Disabilities. The Convention was trumpeted in the United States by the Obama Administration, but is not yet adopted. It seems now to be at the back of the back shelf in federal priorities. This can and should change.

A third pathway is to tackle our current federal and state statutes. The federal books have a plethora of statutes, some overlapping, and some with standards which are inconsistent with one another (including, for example, definitions of disability or eligibility for coverage). We need consolidation and simplification. On the state law front, advocates have been creative using state constitutions and state laws to further disability justice; these efforts should be encouraged.

Another pathway, I suggest, will encompass universal design. Universal design has become a basis for creation of new products, buildings, and environments accessible to everyone with or without disabilities. Mandating universal design would solve many of the issues we confront.

Cultural change is the final pathway to which I commend attention. Many of the essays in this volume see culture change as an essential underpinning to advances for people with disabilities. In my view, seeking such change requires a significantly refined articulation of our goals. Are we talking about accommodation? Inclusion? Assimilation? Disability justice advocates will need to pay increased attention to

---

[7] The influential footnote 4 in *United States v. Carolene Products Co.*, 304 U.S. 144 (1938), stated that there should be heightened scrutiny under the Constitution for particular minorities, those subject to prejudice or with a special condition. Such situations may call for a correspondingly more searching judicial inquiry. Disability discrimination fits within that rubric. *See Carolene Products and Constitutional Structure*, 2013 Sup. Ct. Rev. 321 (2012); *See* Gilman, *The Famous Footnote Four: A History of the Carolene Products Footnote*, 46 S. Tex. L. Rev. 163 (2004); Ferleger, *supra* note 6.

defining our direction as the issues and competing solutions become more nuanced.

The essays in this volume delve into the past, examine the present, and anticipate various futures for achieving disability justice. Understandably, some authors are optimistic, and others question the scope or possibility of future progress. A number of authors present their own experiences in earlier civil rights movements as models and inspiration for the work they do now. Some speak to the issues from the perspective of their own experience as people with disabilities.

One piece of the future appears clear. Despite the unknowns, we know now that we are in the midst of changing a system which sent people with disabilities to separate places, to enter at the back door, to the end of the line.[8] As a distinguished jurist, who happens to be blind, has said, the demand today is for "front door justice."

What is the future of disability justice? We cannot count on the past, even past successes, as harbingers of the future. Those successes might block our visions of the future. Only our imagination and creativity, and our actions, will unlock the future.

---

[8] A cautionary note is appropriate regarding "deinstitutionalization" which ought to go hand in hand with development of "most integrated" (the phrase is from *Olmstead*) community homes for people. Sometimes, the community has replicated undesirable features of the institution.

Seeds of the Past Shaping the Future

Making the Future:
What We Decide to Do as People with Disabilities

Mark Riccobono[1]

My thinking about the future of disability begins with consideration of the important forces influencing society's view of disability. There is no doubt in my mind that the single most important influence on the future of disabilities will be what we decide to do as people with disabilities, to test the perceived limits that society has placed on us, to raise expectations, and to raise expectations for our participation in the world. The keys to our success in the next twenty-five years will be to continue to measure our progress, not by how far we have come, but rather, by how our role in society compares to that of our nondisabled peers, to challenge ourselves and our own assumptions about disability, and the policies that we used to confront the artificial barriers that stand between us and our dreams.

With that in mind, as a spark to the ideas that we will forge together in the years to come, I want to share a few thoughts on just two aspects of the future of disability: education and technological innovation.

I graduated from high school twenty years ago. In many ways, my educational experience as a blind student in the public schools of Milwaukee, Wisconsin, was second class at best. Is education for students with disabilities better today than it was when I was in school? Although I have personally spent much of that twenty years working on the education of blind children, I reluctantly conclude that as a whole, the education for our students is not better today.

---

[1] Mark Riccobono is President of the National Federation of the Blind. Prior to becoming President, he served as executive director of the National Federation of the Blinds Jernigan Institute.

My daughter is now approaching her fifth birthday. She has the same eye condition that I have and is experiencing the same level of blindness as I did when I was five years old. Her younger sister is almost three. She is on that same path. My five-year-old is in pre-K, attending a public charter school in Baltimore City. Her mom and I are not exactly what you would call average parents of a student with a disability. We both have advanced college degrees and extensive advocacy backgrounds on top of experience as blind individuals educated in public schools. We also have a tremendous network of friends across the country who can fill in any of the gaps.

Yet when we showed up at that first IEP meeting, we were immediately met with low expectations that we continue to combat. Although we were able to convince the school to agree to provide instruction in Braille due to our informed advocacy, the teacher of blind students suggested that a reasonable initial accommodation for my daughter would be that she knows the Braille characters for the twenty-six letters of the alphabet with 90 percent accuracy during the first year. It would be no surprise to any of you that the sighted pre-K students are not expected to know anything less than 100 percent of the alphabet by the end of the year. For the child with a disability in our education system today, the bar is automatically set lower based only on the rationale that disability means "lesser than."

The reality is that lower expectations will always reap lower returns. Consider what would have happened, what my daughter's fate would have been, had she had the typical set of parents, individuals who do not have experience with disability, who are not connected with education and advocacy resources like those available in the National Federation of the Blind, and who cling to the hope that the wise special education establishment will give their child the education they do not know how to provide.

The future of disability includes breaking out of today's entrenched notion of special education and creating a revolutionary notion that our twenty-first century classrooms and educators should be tuned to raise expectations for all students. New models of teaching must emerge in which educators with expertise in specific areas of disabilities can work collaboratively with our best subject area educators to unlock the potential of all students.

Schools must stop purchasing inaccessible technology with the goal of later offering what turns out to be an unreasonable accommodation for students with disabilities. We imagine a future where schools will solely implement innovative technologies that are fully usable, regardless of the student's mode of accessing information—auditory, tactile, visual—and regardless of the student's means of manipulating the systems—physical, by voice, or simply by thinking. In that future, our schools will also rely more on authentic mentoring experiences from adults living their lives with disabilities rather than attempting to teach certain skills from a nondisabled perspective.

In order to achieve this future, we are going to have to consider changes to our concept of educational equality for students with disabilities. The Individuals with Disabilities Education Act has been effective in getting our students into classrooms, but it has not provided an equal environment, and it has not significantly transformed the way disability is understood by our best educators. Instead of segregating students with disabilities into specialized classrooms, we have segregated them into integrated classrooms with a special form of education. The end result is largely the same.

The future of disability in education will largely depend on our success in altering the patterns of education for the next generation, and getting people with disabilities to be a more significant driver for educational training, research, and curriculum development.

The degree to which technology is built with accessibility from the beginning will be a critical factor in the future of disability. Equally as important is our success in anticipating the questions that will arise from technology as it becomes more tightly integrated into every aspect of our daily life.

An important illustration is seen in providing greater access to transportation for the disabled. One of the benefits promoted by engineers working on self-driving cars is the great promise of the social benefit to the disabled. Will that be enough to ensure accessibility if the design is baked in?

My belief is that our active advocacy will be required if the promise is to be more than just marketing. There are many policy questions that will arise from shifting from today's concept of drivers to tomorrow's concept of active navigators of self-driving vehicles. Will a license be required? What will the qualifications be? What physical requirements will there be? And how will they be demonstrated? If we allow the decisions to be made by today's pool of eligible drivers and all of the misconceptions that they bring with their experience, we can assume many people with disabilities will be left out. Certainly blind people will be left behind if the expression for poor driving, "What, are you blind?," is any indication.

Our requirements for navigating self-driving cars need to be informed by an authentic view of disability and enriched by our experience, rather than limited by the artificial barriers that have previously existed.

Beyond the policy implications, the physical vehicles of the future will need to include accessibility features. What will the inside of these vehicles be like? Will they allow for access for people with physical disabilities? How will the vehicles be controlled? Will they include inaccessible touch screens? Or will they include built-in accessibility, allowing for information and controls to be accessed and activated through a variety of modalities?

Furthermore, if a self-driving car is built without accessibility features, will it be illegal to sell it in the marketplace? Or will the future of disability mean our riding in the self-driving vehicles that look more like the yellow buses of old, while everybody else is riding in the sleek, sporty vehicles of tomorrow?

The future of disability, in this realm and others, will be determined by our active engagement in these emerging products and our ability to influence design and policy in a society that increasingly values technological innovation. We cannot assume that the advances in technology will either benefit us or be built with us in mind, unless we continue to drive the future of disability.

Education and technical advancement are just two of the domains where we need concentrated action. Employment, parental rights, community involvement, voting, and hundreds of other aspects of our society require our attention.

We can be filled with hope for the future. We need to continue to build skills, and acquire knowledge, which equip us to be proactive and allow us to sharpen our skills in raising expectations to meet that future, to raise expectations, and to overcome the barriers that stand between people with disabilities and our dream.

Disability, the Law of the Poor and the Future

Marc Maurer[1]

In contemplating the shape of disability law twenty-five years in the future, two forces are primary. One of these is the attitude within society regarding the importance of people who possess disabilities. This attitude will inevitably be reflected within the statutes adopted by legislative bodies. The second is the attitude of those who have disabilities with respect to society and the decision-making, which arises from this attitude. If this decision-making is sufficiently bold, the attitude of society will change, and the laws will be modified accordingly. People who have disabilities must be prepared to assume positions of leadership in shaping the law of the future. In other words, contemplation of the nature of the law in the future is more a matter for decision than prediction.

A principle of American law is that it applies equally to all people all of the time. The famous statement of John Adams is that ours is "a government of laws, not of men."[2] However, one of the characteristics of law is that it classifies and categorizes the people to whom it applies. If we know the classification to which you belong, we know what rights you have and how you may be treated. One of the classifications is poverty. Beginning in the 1500s, during the reign of Henry VIII, the British government (which gave the United States its form of jurisprudence) adopted laws directed toward the relief of the poor.[3]

---

[1] Dr. Marc Maurer of Baltimore, Maryland, is immediate past president of the National Federation of the Blind.

[2] John Adams, *The Works of John Adams, Second President of the United States* 106 (Charles Francis Adams ed., Little, Brown & Co., 1856), available at http://oll.libertyfund.org/titles/2102.

[3] Paul Slack, *The English Poor Law*, 1531-1782 (Cambridge University Press, 1995).

In 1601, during the reign of Elizabeth I, Parliament adopted the Act for the Relief of the Poor, a compilation of many of the provisions regarding the poor, which had been adopted earlier; it was a provision to institute a tax for the poor.[4] The ostensible purpose of the Act, as its title suggests, was to provide relief for the poor, but the mechanism of the law was to establish institutions in which those who might otherwise have been beggars on the streets, or vagrants, could be required to work—often at menial trades. Some writers have declared that the jail and the workhouse were the same place.[5] Under Elizabethan law, those who would not work could be punished for not doing so.[6]

In 1966 Dr. Jacobus tenBroek wrote, "Not all who are poor are physically handicapped; not all who are handicapped are poor."[7] However, the coincidence of poverty and unemployment of the blind is enormous. To illustrate this coincidence Dr. tenBroek stated that less than 10 percent of blind Americans receiving Aid to the Blind were employed.[8] Furthermore, Dr. tenBroek also asserted that there are two forms of law: one for the wealthy and one for the poor.[9] The law that

---

[4] The Poor Relief Act, 1601, 43 Eliz., c. 2 (Eng.).

[5] Jacobus tenBroek, *California's Dual System of Family Law: Its Origin, Development, and Present Status*, 16 Stan. L. Rev. 257, 316 (1964).

[6] Jacobus tenBroek & Floyd W. Matson, *Hope Deferred: Public Welfare and the Blind* 40 (University of California Press, 1959).

[7] Jacobus tenBroek & Floyd W. Matson, *The Disabled and the Law of Welfare*, 54 Calif. L. Rev. 809, 809 (1966).

[8] Jacobus tenBroek & Floyd W. Matson, *The Disabled and the Law of Welfare*, 54 Calif. L. Rev. 809, 810 (1966) ("[I]t remains a fact that only a very small fraction—perhaps five or six percent at most—of those with serious physical handicaps are gainfully employed in ordinary open occupations, with an additional two or three percent at work in specially subsidized sheltered employment."); U.S. Census Bureau, *American FactFinder*, 2013 American Community Survey Table B18130, http://factfinder.census.gov/ (last visited March 11, 2015) (The Census Bureau's 2013 American Community Survey contains a table which expresses a statistic that may indicate substantial progress from the time that Dr. tenBroek was writing. This document indicates that 28.7 percent of persons with disabilities aged 18 through 64 are below the federally-established poverty level.)

[9] Jacobus tenBroek, *California's Dual System of Family Law: Its Origin, Development, and Present Status*, 16 Stan. L. Rev. 257, 258 (1964).

applies to people with disabilities is shaped in part by the categorization arising from the law of the poor.

The Rehabilitation Act, the Individuals with Disabilities Education Act, and the Americans with Disabilities Act are not based upon identical legal theories, but they have characteristics in common.

Consider, for example, the Rehabilitation Act.[10] The Poor Law adopted during the time of Queen Elizabeth I established the principle that poor relief would be based upon individual needs, individually determined by a parish official. Relief could be granted only if an official believed the persons receiving it deserved to get it. The statute did not offer an entitlement to the poor. The Rehabilitation Act takes the same approach. Each client is offered the opportunity to create an Individualized Plan for Employment,[11] but the practice in most jurisdictions is to limit this plan by arguments that demand of each client that money be saved on every aspect of rehabilitation.[12] Only the least expensive access technology can be provided; only the junior college can be made available because the expense will be less than that associated with a four-year institution; freedom of choice offers the opportunity to receive orientation and adjustment training at any center of the client's choosing, but the least expensive state-run training program must be used to save funds. The test is not what will work best for the client, but what will be cheapest for the administration. The Rehabilitation Act authorizes the provision of many services but guarantees none of them. Clients do not have the right to training. Rather, they have the right to complain if the training program is inadequate. Requiring this process of the clients ensures not a successful rehabilitation outcome but a continuance of the client in poverty.

---

[10] Rehabilitation Act of 1973, 29 U.S.C. §§ 701-793.

[11] 29 U.S.C. § 722.

[12] *See, e.g., Wasser v. New York State Office of Vocational & Educ. Servs. for Individuals with Disabilities*, 373 F. App'x 120, 121 (2d Cir. 2010); *Yochim v. Gargano*, 882 F. Supp. 2d 1068, 1073 (S.D. Ind. 2012); *Truss v. State, Dep't of Human Servs.*, No. M199901317COAR3CV, 1999 WL 1072583, at *2-5 (Tenn. Ct. App. Nov. 30, 1999).

The Individuals with Disabilities Education Act has a similar philosophy.[13] Each student is guaranteed an Individualized Education Plan, which offers the student a Free Appropriate Public Education. Although the language of the Act suggests that this plan is to be tailored to the individual needs of the student, convenience for the administration is more often the standard employed than success for the student. Decisions interpreting the Act declare that specific services are not guaranteed. Students get "appropriate educational benefits." No standard of excellence is required. The law does not guarantee service. Rather, it guarantees the right to complain if the services wanted are not available.[14]

The Americans with Disabilities Act[15] does guarantee something— at least in theory. Although it does not prohibit paying disabled workers less than the federal minimum wage, this Act says that discrimination based on disability is prohibited, and it offers a method for challenging discrimination. However, the Supreme Court has declared that the protections of this Act do not extend to compensation in the form of money damages paid by states.[16] People who possess disabilities are not classified among those who may expect payment from state governments when discrimination occurs. Furthermore, the special classification of the disabled includes a heavy emphasis on safety. A person possessing a disability may be refused employment if there is a perception that the environment of the job will be a threat to that person's safety.[17] Disabled people do not have the same rights of participation that others possess.

I think the law must adopt the fundamental principle that when you pay for something you are entitled to get it. This principle should apply whether the individual pays directly or has somebody else make the payment. I think the law should abandon the practice of adopting rights

---

[13] Individuals with Disabilities Education Act, 20 U.S.C. §§ 1400-1485.

[14] *Bd. of Educ. of Hendrick Hudson Cent. Sch. Dist., Westchester Cnty. v. Rowley*, 458 U.S. 176, 187-209 102 S. Ct. 3034, 3041-3052 (1982).

[15] Americans with Disabilities Act, 42 U.S.C. §§ 12101-12213.

[16] *Bd. of Trustees of Univ. of Alabama v. Garrett*, 531 U.S. 356, 360, 121 S. Ct. 955, 960 (2001).

[17] *Chevron U.S.A. Inc. v. Echazabal*, 536 U.S. 73, 76-87, 122 S. Ct. 2045, 2047-2054 (2002).

for disabled people without creating a corresponding set of remedies. When I was in law school I learned of the concept of rights without remedies, and I was shocked. What value is a right that cannot be enforced? I wondered. We are paying for rehabilitation; it seems to me that we have a right to get it. We are paying for education; I think we have the right to get that also. The educational experiences offered to disabled people in the United States are severely restricted. This is a form of discrimination. The Americans with Disabilities Act should apply, and the remedies should offer enough revenue to pay for an equal education. These remedies should apply not just to private entities but also to programs within government.

The law of the rich stands for the proposition that those who do not provide the goods and services for which payment has been made face substantial damages or go to jail. The law should be at least as useful to the poor as it is to the rich. We know that those who misrepresent in the securities industry, in banking, and in selling property must pay reparation for the damage they do. We need a change in classification for disabled people so that the law of the rich applies. Those with disabilities have talent, and we should have as much right to use it as anybody else. These are the objectives we must seek to have incorporated in the law within the next twenty-five years.

People with Disabilities:
The Orphan Minority

Fredric K. Schroeder, PhD[1]

The Civil Rights Movement

March 25, 2015, marked the fiftieth anniversary of the third and final Selma to Montgomery civil rights march of 1965. The first was held on March 7, and is, perhaps, the most infamous of the three. The march came to be known as "Bloody Sunday" after six hundred demonstrators were turned back less than a mile into the march at the Edmund Pettus Bridge when state troopers and county posse attacked the unarmed marchers with billy clubs and tear gas.

The demonstrators had set out to walk the fifty-four miles from Selma to the Alabama state capital of Montgomery to draw attention to pervasive racist practices that unlawfully and unfairly limited the right of African-American citizens to exercise their constitutional right to vote. While the demonstrators paid a high price to win their rights, their efforts proved effective. Their sacrifices were rewarded when the Voting Rights Act was adopted by the Congress later that same year. But that was 1965.

Just one year earlier the Congress had passed the Civil Rights Act of 1964. So why were African-American people demonstrating for voting rights? Did not the Civil Rights Act of 1964 already protect them?

Civil rights leaders, including the Reverend Dr. Martin Luther King, Jr., understood that the attainment of equality is not an event

---

[1] Fredric K. Schroeder is a research professor with the San Diego State University Research Foundation.

but a slow and often agonizing, frequently discouraging struggle of people working to emerge from subjugation to equal status. It is the process of changing the hearts and minds of the dominant society. It has transformative moments, but neither its beginning nor its end is fixed in time. In Dr. King's words: "Let us therefore continue our triumphant march to the realization of the American dream."[2]

Unquestionably, the Civil Rights Act of 1964 was a pivotal event in the struggle of African Americans to attain their civil rights; however it was, by no means, the first nor only federal action taken to end racial discrimination and its malignant and corrosive consequences.

It can be argued that the slow and torturous journey to gain civil rights began a century earlier with the abolition of slavery. On January 1, 1863, President Abraham Lincoln issued the Emancipation Proclamation and declared: "all persons held as slaves" within the rebellious states, "are, and henceforward shall be free."[3] But, paradoxically, the Emancipation Proclamation did not free everyone. Slaves were granted freedom, but freedom was only for slaves living in states that had seceded from the Union. In the loyal Border States the right of white people to hold black people in bondage continued.

The struggle for equal status began when American slaves were freed, but it took over a century before the inherent equality of African-American people would be affirmed in law. The Emancipation Proclamation of 1863 and the Civil Rights Act of 1964 were not unrelated, dissociated independent events; they marked distinct, transformative moments in a social evolution, the painstakingly slow social awakening of the human consciousness and conscience to face injustice and to acknowledge the humanity of all people.

---

[2]   Carson, C., & Shepard, K., (Eds.). (2001). *A Call to Conscience: The Landmark Speeches of Dr. Martin Luther King, Jr.* New York: IPM/Warner Books. Retrieved from http://mlk-kpp01.stanford.edu/index.php/ kingpapers/article/ our_god_is_marching_on/

[3]   Emancipation Proclamation, January 1, 1863; Presidential Proclamations, 1791-1991; Record Group 11; General Records of the United States Government; National Archives. Retrieved from http://www.archives.gov/exhibits/ featured_documents/emancipation_proclamation/transcript.html

The Emancipation Proclamation was not the end but the beginning. Soon thereafter, on December 6, 1865, the Thirteenth Amendment to the Constitution of the United States of America abolished slavery and involuntary servitude, except as punishment for a crime. Eight years later, the Congress enacted the Civil Rights Act of 1871, also known as the Ku Klux Klan Act. The act granted to the President the authority to suspend the writ of habeas corpus to combat the Ku Klux Klan and the other white supremacy organizations during the Reconstruction Era. The tide of history seemed to be moving toward integration at a steady and heartening rate.

But then followed the Civil Rights Act of 1875, prohibiting discrimination in hotels, trains, and other public facilities, an important milestone, but one that would soon be challenged. At first all seemed to be well. In 1877 the Supreme Court ruled in *Hall v. DeCuir* that the states could not enforce segregation on common carriers such as railroads, streetcars, or riverboats. While a dramatic victory for African Americans, the court decision proved to be too much for whites to bear. The slaves were free, but the South continued to enforce strict separation of the races. Freedom was one thing, but equality was quite another.

The constitutionality of the 1875 Civil Rights Act continued to come under fire. In 1883 the court overturned key protections of the Civil Rights Act of 1875, thereby laying the foundation for the idea of "separate but equal," although the term was not introduced at that time. But more was to follow. Seven years later the court approved a Mississippi statute requiring segregation on intrastate carriers in *Louisville, New Orleans & Texas Railway v. Mississippi* (1890).[4]

During the years 1887 to 1892 nine states passed laws requiring separation of the races on public conveyances, such as streetcars and railroads. Segregation of the races was viewed to be natural and not discriminatory. The Louisiana Separate Car Act of 1890 included the language that, in order to "promote the comfort of passengers," railroads had to provide "equal but separate accommodations for the white and colored races" on lines running in the state.

---

[4] *Louisville, New Orleans & Texas Railway v. Mississippi*, 133 U.S. 587 (1890).

Even in the face of defeat after defeat, proponents of racial equality somehow managed to maintain their spirit and fight back. On June 7, 1892, Homer Plessy walked into the Press Street Depot in New Orleans, bought a first-class ticket to Covington, and boarded the East Louisiana Railroad's Number 8 train. When ordered to move, Homer Plessy refused. "I am an American citizen," he told the trainman. "I have paid for a first-class ticket, and intend to ride to Covington in the first-class car."[5] Plessy was arrested and charged with violating the Separate Car Act. A long series of court battles followed.

On May 18, 1896, the U.S. Supreme Court ruled against Plessy, heralding seven decades of what came to be known as the Jim Crow era, a period in American history infamous for perpetuating the presumed legitimacy of racial segregation.[6] But, eventually the injustice of segregation would be challenged, and the tide would begin to turn.

The Civil Rights Act of 1957 created the Civil Rights Commission. Then the Civil Rights Act of 1960 established federal inspection of local voter registration polls.

Then followed what was unarguably the most significant declaration of human rights of the twentieth century: the Civil Rights Act of 1964. The Civil Rights Act prohibited discrimination based on race, color, religion, sex, and national origin by federal and state governments as well as some public places. But the passage of the Civil Rights Act did not end the struggle for equality. Just one year later, Congress passed the Voter Rights Act of 1965.

Reflecting on the events leading to the passage of the Voter Rights Act, the Reverend Dr. Martin Luther King said:

> . . . today as I stand before you and think back over that great march, I can say, as Sister Pollard said—a seventy-year-old Negro woman who lived in this community during the bus boycott—and one day, she was asked

---

[5] Jim Crow law. (2015). *In Encyclopedia Britannica*. Retrieved from http://www.britannica.com/EBchecked/topic/303897/Jim-Crow-law/324448/Homer-Plessy-and-Jim-Crow

[6] *Plessy v. Ferguson*, 163 U.S. 537 (1896).

while walking if she didn't want to ride. And when she answered, 'No,' the person said, 'Well, aren't you tired?' And with her ungrammatical profundity, she said, 'My feets is tired, but my soul is rested.' And in a real sense this afternoon, we can say that our feet are tired, but our souls are rested.

Dr. King went on to say: "The Civil Rights Act of 1964 gave Negroes some part of their rightful dignity, but without the vote it was dignity without strength."

Three years later the Congress enacted the Civil Rights Act of 1968, also known as the Fair Housing Act, to be followed by the Civil Rights Act of 1991, providing the right to trial by jury on discrimination claims and introducing the possibility of emotional distress damages, although the law limited the amount that a jury could award. And the struggle for equality is not over; it will not be over until African Americans and other minority groups are regarded as equals, treated as equals, and are able to live free from discrimination.

Civil Rights and Disability Rights

But how do we address the civil rights for people with disabilities? If people with disabilities suffer discrimination based on prejudice and preconception, then it logically follows that people with disabilities, like other disenfranchised people, deserve to have their civil rights consecrated in law. But society does not regard the prejudice people with disabilities face as comparable to the discrimination faced by other members of minority groups.

By definition disability means a loss of mental or physical function, but its social construction encompasses much more. Society regards disability not just as a limitation in sight, hearing, mobility or mental or intellectual functioning, but as a condition of generalized defect and damage. While it is recognized that people with disabilities face discrimination, it is quietly yet firmly believed that the limited opportunity they face is at least in equal degree the inevitable, inescapable consequence of their infirmity.

So, what about civil rights protections for people with disabilities? Twenty-five years ago, the Congress passed the Americans with Disabilities Act (ADA), landmark legislation affirming the right of people with disabilities to live free from discrimination. There is no question that the ADA transformed America's thinking about disability and the rights of people with disabilities. But when we compare the protections contained in the ADA to those contained in the Civil Rights Act of 1964, we find a number of dramatic and disappointing differences.

While the ADA prohibits employment discrimination based on disability, it is a limited prohibition. Specifically, the ADA forbids employment discrimination against people with disabilities but only to those individuals who are deemed to be a "qualified individual." People with disabilities are protected from employment discrimination, but not all people with disabilities. Only the "qualified," the worthy, only those people with disabilities who do not cost too much to accommodate or are not too much bother. People with disabilities are minorities, but they are an orphan minority, a subordinate minority. People with disabilities have some civil rights protections, but not the same protections afforded to ethnic minorities and other protected classes of individuals.

In barring discrimination against other minority individuals, it is striking to note that the term "qualified individual" is not contained in Title VII of the Civil Rights Act of 1964. The act simply says, "It shall be an unlawful employment practice for an employer … to discriminate against any individual with respect to his compensation, terms, conditions, or privileges of employment, because of such individual's race, color, religion, sex, or national origin." (Title VII, Civil Rights Act of 1964 Sec. 703(a)(1) or 42 USC 2000e-2(a)(1))

The Civil Rights Act makes no mention of a "qualified individual from a specified ethnic background," no mention of a "qualified woman," no mention of a "qualified member of a defined religious faith," and no mention of a "qualified individual of a particular national origin." While not explicitly stated, it is assumed that people are not inherently inferior by virtue of race, color, religion, sex or national origin. In other words, it is understood that they are inherently normal people, capable people, people whose lives are unjustly constricted by prejudice. They are not required to prove that they are qualified, because they are assumed to be qualified; they are assumed to be equal in capacity and ability. They are not made infirm nor limited by their minority status but by prejudice. But the same is not assumed to be true for people with disabilities. The idea of barring employment discrimination against people with disabilities is reserved to those people with disabilities who are deemed to be "qualified."

The ADA states: "(a) General rule: No covered entity shall discriminate against a qualified individual on the basis of disability in regard to job application procedures, the hiring, advancement, or discharge of employees, employee compensation, job training, and other terms, conditions, and privileges of employment." (42 U.S.C. § 12112(a)).

But what makes a person with a disability qualified? What is the standard that divides the able from the unable? The ADA defines the term qualified individual with a disability as follows:

> (8) Qualified individual. The term "qualified individual" means an individual who, with or without reasonable accommodation, can perform the essential functions of the employment position that such individual holds or desires. For the purposes of this subchapter, consideration shall be given to the employer's judgment as to what functions of a job are essential, and if an employer has prepared a written description before advertising or interviewing applicants for the job, this description shall be considered evidence of the essential functions of the job. (42 U.S.C. § 12111(8)).

So, not all people with disabilities are protected from employment discrimination. The individual with a disability must first show that he or she is a "qualified person." And who decides whether the individual is qualified, able to perform the essential functions of the job? As we see, the ADA states that "…consideration shall be given to the employer's judgment …" People with disabilities are members of a minority group, but their protections are not the same as the protections available to others. People with disabilities are minorities, but they are orphan minorities.

The definition of a qualified individual with a disability is linked to the concept of a "reasonable accommodation." People with disabilities are guaranteed the right to be given accommodations, but not any accommodation, only those deemed to be reasonable. Of course the converse of reasonable is unreasonable, and no one would argue that people with disabilities must have the right to unreasonable accommodations, but the question of what makes an accommodation reasonable is more than a rhetorical flourish, an interesting intellectual exercise; it is foundational.

The distinction between reasonable and unreasonable accommodations is rooted in society's conception that people with disabilities are like and unlike other minority individuals. They face social barriers, but they are equally limited by their own incapacity. While it is kind and fair to grant them accommodations, the accommodations must be reasonable, that is, they must not cost too much or be too much bother or inconvenience. It is a distinction between the worthy and the unworthy. Those people with disabilities who, albeit damaged, can do a little something. It is the benevolence of the master to the ward, the superior to the inferior, the parent to the child. And as with the determination of what constitutes the essential functions of the job, the determination of whether an accommodation is reasonable falls to the employer. Of course the authority of the employer is neither absolute nor unfettered. Still, it is revealing to note that the employer's defense, the employer's standard of proof when challenged is to show that an accommodation is not reasonable because it imposes an "undue hardship" on the employer, that is, it costs too much or is too much bother.

This year we are celebrating the twenty-fifth anniversary of the passage of the ADA–and celebrating we are–but we must do more than celebrate; we must look back on where we were, assess where we are now, and then chart the future. The ADA was a transformative moment in the struggle for equal rights. The legal protections themselves were dramatic, but of greater significance was the long-awaited social awakening that enabled the law to be taken seriously and adopted by the Congress. The progress we have made is worth celebrating, but as we celebrate, we must also look forward. If people with disabilities are to be successful in taking the next step toward equal status, we must secure full and equal civil rights protections in law, and we must line up our programs, services and supports to conform to and sustain the conception of disability as a minority issue, a civil rights issue, a human rights issue. People with disabilities are minorities, but we are not an orphan minority.

Eliminate Subminimum Wages for People with Disabilities

It is time to eliminate Section 14(c) of the Fair Labor Standards Act (FLSA). Section 14(c) grants an exception from the minimum wage requirements under the FLSA. Section 14(c) does incalculable economic harm to people with disabilities, but its corrosive effects go far beyond their impoverishment. Section 14(c) perpetuates society's harmful and unfounded belief that people with disabilities are broken people, damaged people, defective people different from other minorities because their minority status is based on their infirmity, their inability, a condition that renders them less able and less productive than others—an orphan minority, a subordinate minority. The Section 14(c) exception sustains the idea that there are places for those people, people incapable of working alongside others, benevolent places separate and apart from society as a whole.

Federal regulations euphemize subminimum wages. Instead of calling them what they are, subminimum wages, the term commensurate wage is used (29 CFR Part 525). Commensurate wage is defined as "… a special minimum wage paid to a worker with a disability which is based on the worker's individual productivity …. Commensurate wage is always a special minimum wage, i.e., a wage below the statutory minimum."

Seventy-seven years ago this year, as a central piece of the New Deal, President Roosevelt secured passage of the FLSA. Among other protections, the FLSA guaranteed American workers a minimum wage; but not all American workers. From its inception the FLSA excused employers from paying people with disabilities the minimum wage. It was understood that people with disabilities could not be as productive as others, and if employers were required to pay them the minimum wage (at that time twenty-five cents an hour), people with disabilities would not be employed at all.

While neither just nor morally defensible, we understand that in 1938, when the FLSA was passed, no one would have seriously proposed that people with disabilities be included under the minimum wage requirement. Indeed it would have been seen as unkindness, a deepening of the hardships that already defined their lives. No one would pay a person with a disability the minimum wage, so instead of limited opportunities for employment, they would have none. People with disabilities were broken people, damaged people, inferior people. They suffered inferior status through no fault of their own, but they were inferior just the same.

The question is not whether there are people with complex disabilities that impair their productivity; the question is whether it is equitable and just to require people with disabilities to prove their worth and to do so by performing mind-numbing, repetitive work. People with disabilities are not given menial, monotonous work because it is the only work they can do but because it is work that fits society's low expectations. It makes no sense to take a class of people, people who have a limitation in a physical or mental function, and constrict the number of jobs available to them. Objectively, one would think that people with disabilities need access to the widest number of employment options to facilitate a good match between the individual and the job. But beyond the objective flaw in the paradigm, the Section 14(c) exemption perpetuates discrimination; it reinforces the idea that people with disabilities are damaged, limited people—an orphan minority. It is time to cut the Gordian Knot and eliminate this vestige of a shameful past. It is time—past time—to repeal Section 14(c) of the FLSA.

Reform the Javits-Wagner-O'Day Act Program to Support Integrated, Competitive Employment

The AbilityOne Commission administers the Javits–Wagner-O'Day (JWOD) Act 41 U.S.C. Section 46 et seq. The AbilityOne Commission (known in law as the Committee for Purchase from People Who Are Blind or Severely Disabled) grants noncompetitive contracts to nonprofit community rehabilitation programs (CRPs) that provide specified supplies and services to agencies of the federal government. The qualified CRPs employ people who are blind or who have other significant disabilities. The act was passed by the 92nd United States Congress in 1971 and has not been amended or updated since that time.

Last year the AbilityOne Commission allotted approximately $2.8 billion in noncompetitive federal contracts to CRPs that employ people with disabilities. To work on these contracts, an individual must be legally blind or must have a physical or mental disability that "constitutes a substantial handicap to employment and is of such a nature as to prevent the individual under such disability from currently engaging in normal competitive employment."[7] But who decides that an individual is incapable of engaging in "normal competitive employment"? The CRP does. And who decides the individual's productivity? The CRP does. And who decides how many hours an individual will work each week? The CRP does. And who oversees the program? Essentially no one. The program has been plagued by countless abuses arising, in large part, from the inherent conflicts of interest that comprise the structure of the JWOD program.

JWOD federal contracts are used to support segregated work settings that often pay wages below the prevailing wage or minimum wage. The wages are kept low, and the number of work hours is limited to protect Social Security disability benefits. As a result, the JWOD program helps sustain low wage employment in segregated settings.

The JWOD program should be updated to direct the purchasing power of the federal government to support equitable pay and integration. The following are four specific recommendations that would transform the JWOD program from one that works against integration into a program that fosters high wages, dignity, and self-support.

First, the JWOD program should be conceptualized as a disability employment program, not as a federal procurement program. At present the majority of the federal agency representatives to the AbilityOne Commission are senior procurement officers. While the AbilityOne Commission includes public members and customarily

---

[7] Javits-Wagner-O'Day Act of 1971, 41 U.S.C. 8501-8506. Retrieved from http://www.abilityone.gov/laws_and_regulations/jwod.html

the Commissioner of the Rehabilitation Services Administration, the program is largely guided by people with no knowledge or background in disability employment programs. The administration of the AbilityOne program should be moved to an agency such as the Rehabilitation Services Administration within the U.S. Department of Education or the Office of Disability Employment Policy within the U.S. Department of Labor.

Second, eligibility for the program should be based on a determination that the individual meets the Social Security Administration's definition of disability. The individual would not need to be receiving SSI or SSDI benefits, only meet the disability portion of the program's eligibility criteria. The CRPs should not be allowed to determine the severity of the individual's disability. By law, eligibility for the program is reserved to those individuals with disabilities that are so significant that they are unable to work in competitive settings. At present there is a direct conflict of interest since it is the CRP that determines the severity of the individual's disability, and hence, who is accepted for inclusion in the program. It is in the interest of the CRPs to qualify individuals who have minimal levels of disability, so the CRPs' workforce is as productive as possible. This flies in the face of the act's purpose and intent.

Third, noncompetitive JWOD federal contracts should not be used to support subminimum wages for people with disabilities. JWOD contracts are given to nonprofit agencies that receive an array of governmental and philanthropic subsidies to provide employment for people with disabilities. It is unfair and unjust to allow the CRPs to determine the productivity of an individual since it is the CRP that stands to benefit by constricting the wages of its workers. The JWOD program should be used to support wages that enable people with disabilities to be self-supporting and to attain a decent standard of living, not to perpetuate penury and isolation.

Fourth, the JWOD program should limit contracts to work in integrated settings. This would require a thoughtful and planned transition, but it is something that is long overdue.

Eliminate the Earnings Limits for the Social Security Disability Programs

It is time to eliminate the earnings limit for the Social Security Disability Insurance (SSDI) and the Supplemental Security Income (SSI) programs. The earnings limits serve to keep people with disabilities in perpetual poverty and dependent on public programs to meet the costs associated with their disability.

Although the Social Security Administration (SSA) applies a strict definition of disability, monthly benefits are not paid to all people who meet the SSA definition of disability. The SSDI program pays benefits only to those individuals whose earnings, if any, are below the threshold known as "Substantial Gainful Activity" (SGA) (in 2015, $1,090 for disabled beneficiaries and $1,820 for blind beneficiaries). It has been known for many years that SSDI beneficiaries limit their income to stay below the SGA earnings limit, thereby protecting their SSDI benefits.

The SSI program operates under somewhat different rules than the SSDI program; however both penalize work and lead to chronic poverty for individuals with disabilities (monthly payment amounts for the SSI program in 2015: $733 for an eligible individual, $1,100 for an eligible individual with an eligible spouse, and $367 for an essential person).

But why limit the earnings of individuals who receive SSI or SSDI benefits at all? Conceptually, both programs reflect a welfare model, that is, they presume that, once an individual has demonstrated his or her ability to work, the taxpayer should no longer supplement the individual's income. What they fail to recognize is that people with disabilities incur costs throughout their lifetime related to their disability. The welfare model of disability income support assumes that either the individual will be able to pay his or her disability related costs or a public program will assist or the individual will have to make due the best he or she can. This leaves the person with a disability either without needed services or as a perpetual ward of the state.

From a disability rights standpoint, the threshold question is whether the cost of disability should be borne by the individual or whether it should be distributed across society as a whole. There are many examples of distributed costs: we are asked to pay taxes to support public schools, irrespective of whether we have school-age children; we are asked to pay for police, even if we do not directly use the service. It is recognized that schools and police benefit society generally, and their costs should be shared.

But perhaps a better example is road maintenance. For most of us if the road on which we live needs to be repaired or replaced, tax dollars are used to meet the expense. No one assesses the ability of each homeowner to pay a portion of the cost, based on the earnings of the individual. The road in front of an individual's house is not used by everyone, but its maintenance is still seen as a legitimate public expense. The same should be true for the costs of disability.

Eliminating the SSDI and SSI earnings limits would immediately end the disincentive to work. By stimulating work activity, more taxes would be paid, and people with disabilities would have the opportunity to attain a better standard of living. But more important, eliminating the earnings limits would mean that people with disabilities would have some money under their direct control to help offset the costs associated with their disability. No applying to charitable or governmental programs; no means testing. The individual would have some money to pay for assistive technology, the cost of hiring a job coach, transportation, and so on. Instead we means test SSDI and SSI recipients each and every month to make sure that they are still unemployed, still poor, and to what end? The Congress acknowledged the self-defeating consequence of limiting work and eliminated the earnings limit for retirees. It is time to do the same for people with disabilities.

End the Conception of Disability as an Orphan Minority

People with disabilities constitute a minority group in every legitimate sense of the word. They face discrimination and have their lives limited by socially constructed barriers to full participation. But their minority status is not regarded as entirely comparable to that of ethnic minorities, people of different colors, religions, faiths or national origins.

While people with disabilities have made significant strides toward true integration, their progress has been suppressed by society's conception of people with disabilities as broken people, damaged people, inferior people. Civil rights are reserved for others while people with disabilities are made to make do with limited civil rights, qualified civil rights, or conditional civil rights. People with disabilities are members of a minority group, but it is an orphan minority, a subordinate minority.

The ADA was a transformative moment in the struggle of people with disabilities for equal status, but as with the Civil Rights Act of 1964, it did not end the struggle for true equality. Equality will not be an event, a moment of social awakening. It will take years, generations, each building on the foundation laid by those who came before. It is fair, even compulsory, to take heart from what we have achieved, but the struggle must continue, continue until people with disabilities take their rightful place as equals among equals.

Conclusion

In the words of Nelson Mandela: "I have walked that long road to freedom. I have tried not to falter; I have made missteps along the way. But I have discovered the secret that, after climbing a great hill, one only finds that there are many more hills to climb. I have taken a moment here to rest, to steal a view of the glorious vista that surrounds me, to look back on the distance I have come. But I can only rest for a moment, for with freedom come responsibilities, and I dare not linger, for my long walk is not ended."[8]

The same is true for people with disabilities. We must stand up against injustice; we must stand up against isolation, and we must never falter. As days become weeks and weeks become months, and as months become years and years become decades, we must not lose heart. Humanity demands it; decency demands it; and justice demands it. We are not an orphan minority; we are not damaged people, lesser people. We are people, people with our own individual abilities, interests, and dreams. We are people deserving of full and equal civil rights, full and equal opportunity, and the human dignity that is the right of all people.

---

[8]   Mandela, N., (1994). *Long Walk to Freedom: The Autobiography of Nelson Mandela.* Boston: Little, Brown.

The First "A" in the ADA:
And Twenty-Five More "A"s towards
Equality for Americans with Disabilities

Peter Blanck, PhD, JD[1]

This article accentuates the first "A" in the Americans with Disabilities Act (ADA) of 1990. That first "A" in the ADA's law and policy framework is to apply to *all* qualified individuals with disabilities residing, working, recreating, using the web, and engaged in daily life activities with private and public organizations in the United States[2]

The purpose of the 2015 tenBroek Symposium was to celebrate and take stock of the past twenty-five years of the ADA, and to reflect upon and consider the coming twenty-five years. Certainly, during the last twenty-five years, there have been dramatic changes in the perceptions of disability, from primarily viewing it as a medical state to be cured and pitied toward acceptance of disability as an element of the human experience and self-identity. The ADA's modern understanding of disability is as much shaped by diversity in biology, culture, and self-identity over the life course, as it is by the barriers to inclusion built and still maintained in society. The ADA endorses this paradigm shift from the prior and dominating medical model to a social and environmental approach to disability civil and human rights.

---

[1] Peter Blanck is university professor and chairman, Burton Blatt Institute, Syracuse University, Syracuse, New York.

[2] Blanck, P. (2014). *eQuality: The Struggle for Web Accessibility by Persons with Cognitive Disabilities.* Cambridge, UK: Cambridge University Press.; Schur, L., Kruse, D., & Blanck, P. (2013). *People with Disabilities: Sidelined or Mainstreamed?* Cambridge, UK: Cambridge University Press.

I consider here the significance of the law's past and consider its future. My emphasis on the first "A" in the ADA, as said, provides focus on the individual and the uniquely human lived social experience. In this article, I use the first "A" in the ADA as my starting point to consider twenty-five such "A"s as important to understanding the past and as useful for framing future action. The numbering of these "A"s herein is bold bracketed coinciding with the associated italicized text.

I already have provided my first two "A"s; that is, *Americans* [1] as broadly conceived for purposes of the Act that affects *all* [2] of us, those with visible and non-visible disabilities, older adults who may experience disability as part of the aging process, members of the *Armed Forces* [3] and veterans who have experienced Post Traumatic Stress Disorder (PTSD) and Traumatic Brain Injury (TBI) as signature injuries of recent wars, and the family members, friends, and supporters of these individuals as partners in daily living.

Arithmetic [4] (Demographics)

It is estimated that by the year 2100, the world's population will rise to more than ten billion people, up from the approximately 7.3 billion people today.[3] By that time, the majority of individuals will live in *Asia* [5] and *Africa* [6], and in developing countries, with a predicted rise in poverty throughout the world.[4] An estimated one billion people or fifteen percent of the present world population live with disabilities, comprising the world's largest minority, and that number is expected to rise with medical and technological advances.[5] The *aging* [7] process

---

[3] Current World Population (2015). Retrieved from http://www.worldometers.info/world-population/.; Live Science (2015). Retrieved from http://www.livescience.com/topics/world-population.; United Nations, Department of Economic and Social Affairs, World Population to Exceed 10 Billion (May 5, 2011). Retrieved from http://www.un.org/en/development/desa/news/population/population-exceed-10-billion.html

[4] Pew Research Center, "10 Projections for the Global Population in 2050" (Feb. 3, 2014). Retrieved from http://www.pewresearch.org/fact-tank/2014/02/03/10-projections-for-the-global-population-in-2050/.

[5] United Nations, enable, Factsheet on Persons with Disabilities (2015). Retrieved from http://www.un.org/disabilities/default.asp?id=18.

will further add to a rise in individuals living with disabilities in the coming decades. Individuals are living longer.[6] The U.S. is expected to have among the most significant relative increases in population in the coming decades, with the populations of Japan, South Korea, Russia, and Germany declining.[7] The population of Africa is projected to increase faster than other areas of the world and will constitute a larger share of the global population.[8]

The implications of these demographic shifts are pronounced for individuals with disabilities. For example, older individuals will spend more time living with disabilities, and they may require greater resources to support their aging dependents with disabilities.[9] More individuals in developing countries and regions such as Africa will have disabilities, and many will live in poverty, have lower educational attainment, and experience multiple forms of discrimination on the basis of disability and gender, race, and ethnicity. The United Nations Convention on the Rights of Persons with Disabilities (CRPD), for example, increasingly will address issues of legal capacity (Article 12) for individuals with cognitive impairments across the life span and particularly coinciding with the aging process.[10]

The rising global population will include greater numbers of individuals who have *autism* **[8]**, and print and learning disabilities such as *Attention Deficit Hyperactivity Disorder (ADHD)* **[9]** and *Attention-Deficit Disorder (ADD)* **[10]**. These individuals and others with cognitive

---

[6] Pew Research Center, "10 Projections for the Global Population in 2050" (Feb. 3, 2014). Retrieved from http://www.pewresearch.org/fact-tank/2014/02/03/10-projections-for-the-global-population-in-2050/.

[7] Pew Research Center, "10 Projections for the Global Population in 2050" (Feb. 3, 2014). Retrieved from http://www.pewresearch.org/fact-tank/2014/02/03/10-projections-for-the-global-population-in-2050/.

[8] Pew Research Center, "10 Projections for the Global Population in 2050" (Feb. 3, 2014). Retrieved from http://www.pewresearch.org/fact-tank/2014/02/03/10-projections-for-the-global-population-in-2050/.

[9] United Nations, enable, Factsheet on Persons with Disabilities (2015). Retrieved from http://www.un.org/disabilities/default.asp?id=18.

[10] Blanck, P., & Martinis, J. (2015). "The Right to Make Choices": National Resource Center for Supported Decision-Making. *Inclusion,* 3(1), 24-33.

disabilities continue to face stigma and high levels of discrimination in employment and other activities central to daily life.

Abode [11] (Choosing Where to Live)

In the United States, the ADA's "integration mandate" was affirmed by the Supreme Court in the seminal case *Olmstead v L.C.* (1999). Like its inspiring predecessor in the area of race and equal education *Brown v. Board of Education* (1954), the *Olmstead* decision declared that state-sponsored separate and non-integrated living arrangements were discriminatory toward people with disabilities. *Olmstead* involved the equal right of individuals with cognitive and mental health disabilities to live in the community, as opposed to being segregated in institutions. The decision reflects the paradigm shift in disability rights from acceptance of life in segregated institutions and nursing homes to the right to integrated community living.[11]

Olmstead also rejects the blanket presumption that children with disabilities learning in separate "special" classes equates to mainstream education, as it does that "employment" in segregated sheltered workplaces is equivalent to the opportunity for integrated competitive work at a living wage. In short, as the Supreme Court stated under the ADA, "unjustified isolation . . . is properly regarded as discrimination based on disability."[12]

Nonetheless, in 2015, several prominent ethicists argued that in the U.S. we should "Bring Back the *Asylum*" [12] because in many ways deinstitutionalization for persons with mental disabilities has turned into transinstitutionalization toward nursing homes, general hospitals, prisons, and homelessness.[13] As a former court officer overseeing class

---

[11] McDonald, K., Williamson, P., Weiss, S., Adya, M., & Blanck, P. (2015). The March Goes On: Community Access for People with Disabilities, *Journal of Community Psychology*, 43(3), 348-363.

[12] *Olmstead v. L.C.*, 527 U.S. 581 (1999); Blanck, P. (2014). *eQuality: The struggle for web accessibility by persons with cognitive disabilities.* Cambridge, UK: Cambridge University Press.

[13] Sisti, D., Segal, A., & Emanuel, E. (2015). Improving Long-Term Psychiatric Care: Bring Back the Asylum, *JAMA* 313(3): 243-244.

action litigation in deinstitutionalization and community service development cases for individuals with intellectual disabilities[14] and individuals with serious and persistent mental illness,[15] I can attest to the fact that the ADA's *Olmstead* mandate has changed lives for the better. By its purpose, the slippery slope of institutionalization inevitably leads to less opportunity to flourish in individual growth, rehabilitation, and recovery as documented by the lived experience and empirical study.

Avocation [13] (Employment and Economic Self-Sufficiency for Autonomy) [14]

The Achieving a Better Life Experience (*ABLE*) Act was overwhelmingly approved with bipartisan support by Congress and signed into law by President Obama on December 19, 2014 (*ABLE Act* of 2014) [15]. ABLE amends Section 529 of the Internal Revenue Code to allow use of tax-free savings accounts for eligible individuals with disabilities. But ABLE is more than the establishment of tax-free savings accounts because it represents one of the most significant pieces of legislation since passage of the ADA.[16] ABLE opens new pathways toward independence and economic self-sufficiency for individuals with disabilities and their families.[17] ABLE offers opportunities for individuals with disabilities to lead self-determined and self-directed lives by setting financial savings goals and having friends and family contribute resources to their future.

The need to spur employment and economic self-sufficiency for people with disabilities is apparent, as twenty-five years after ADA

---

[14] *Weston v. Wyoming State Training School*, 2:90-cv-0004-ABJ (D.Wyo. Apr. 27, 1994).

[15] *Chris S. v. Jim Geringer*, 2:94-cv-00311-ABJ (D.Wyo. Dec. 29, 1994). Current World Population (2015). Retrieved from http://www.worldometers.info/world-population/.

[16] Morris, M., Rodriguez, C., & Blanck, P. (2015). ABLE Accounts: A Down Payment on Freedom, *Inclusion* (forthcoming).

[17] Blanck, P. (2015). ADA at 25 and People with Cognitive Disabilities: From Voice to Action, *Inclusion* (forthcoming).

passage there has been little change in employment and economic status for working age adults with disabilities. As said, the poverty rate of people with disabilities in the U.S. is more than double the rate of people without disabilities. These disparities are compounded by higher costs associated with living with a disability, which further associates with fewer and lower quality in life choices of community participation, where to live, and access to transportation and healthcare. The *Affordable Health Care Act* of 2010 **[16]** was created "to increase the number of Americans covered by health insurance and decrease the cost of health care."[18] The U.S. Supreme Court has upheld the constitutionality of the law, along with its goal of Medicaid expansion for individuals with disabilities and those living in poverty to obtain affordable medical care.

For many people with disabilities to attain, maintain, and advance in employment and economic self-sufficiency, Internet technology must be *accessible* **[17]** and usable. My recent book, *eQuality: The Struggle for Web Accessibility by Persons with Cognitive Disabilities* (2014), examined the right under the ADA to full and equal web access for people with disabilities in employment, education, and other areas central to self-advancement. Given the ubiquity of online activity in the United States and most of the world, as well as the shifting of nearly all daily interactions and activities to the Internet, the right under the ADA and other laws to web equality may seem obvious.[19] However, establishing the rights of individuals with disabilities, and in particular of individuals with cognitive disabilities—intellectual and developmental disabilities, autism, traumatic brain injury, and other conditions—has seldom come without legal and political struggle, which also is necessary to achieve a broader shift in attitudes and practice.[20] Web equality, grounded in

---

[18] *National Federation of Independent Business et al., v. Sebelius*, at 2580, 2014

[19] Blanck, P. (2016) *eQuality*: The Right to the Web, in *A Research Companion to Disability Law*. Oxford, UK: Ashgate Companion Series (forthcoming).

[20] Blanck. P. & Marti, M. (1997). Attitudes, Behavior, and the Employment Provisions of the Americans with Disabilities Act, *Villanova L. Rev.*, 42(2), 345-408.

ADA law and policy is necessary for people with disabilities to fully partake and flourish in the information age over the life course.[21]

Workplace *accommodations* [18], such as *assistive technologies* [19] and those for the physical world as mandated by the Americans with Disabilities Act Accessibility Guidelines (*ADAAG*, 2002) [20], often are crucial in efforts to recruit and retain employees with disabilities.[22] In a series of studies, my colleagues and I have examined the provision of workplace accommodations and employers' often unfounded concerns over potential accommodation costs. In 2014, we published the first study to systematically examine workplace accommodations from multiple perspectives—those of employees, co-workers, and managers—and to compare accommodation requests, costs, and benefits between employees with and without disabilities. This study reported on accommodations requested and granted from intensive case studies of eight companies, based on over 5,000 employee and manager surveys, and interviews and focus groups with 128 managers and employees with disabilities.

Consistent with prior research findings, in our comprehensive 2014 study we found that people with disabilities are more likely than those without disabilities to request accommodations, but the types of accommodations requested and the reported costs and benefits are similar for disability and nondisability accommodations. In particular, fears of high accommodation costs and negative reactions of co-workers were not realized. The granting of accommodations also had positive spillover effects on attitudes of co-workers, as well as a positive effect on attitudes of requesting employees, particularly when co-workers were

---

[21] Blanck, P., & Martinis, J. (2015). "The Right to Make Choices": National Resource Center for Supported Decision-Making. *Inclusion*, 3(1), 24-33; Putnam, M. (2014). Bridging Network Divides: Building Capacity to Support Aging with Disability Populations Through Research, *Disability and Health Journal*, 7(1), S51-S59.

[22] Pransky, G., Blanck, P., et al. (2016). The Future of Workplace Accommodation, Improving Research of Employer Practices to Prevent Disability, *Journal of Occupational Rehabilitation* (forthcoming); Schur, L., Nishii, L., Adya, M., Kruse, D., Bruyère, S., & Blanck, P. (2014). Accommodating Employees With and Without Disabilities, *Human Resource Management*, 53(4), 593-621.

supportive. The results point to the benefits from a corporate culture of flexibility and attention to the individualized needs of employees.

Future research is needed, across a variety of large and small work settings, to shed further light on the benefits of workplace accommodations, their effects on organizational culture and employee and employer needs, and how they increase equal employment opportunities for individuals with disabilities. More remains to be learned about individual managerial *attitudes* [21], styles, and leadership qualities that create and maintain workplace climates that maximize productivity and engagement, especially for employees with disabilities.

Advocacy [22] (Voice to Action) [23]

Continued advocacy by persons with disabilities, and their families and supporters, to advance full and equal participation in the world is the foremost means to change attitudes and behavior, and eventually to advance cultural norms.[23] The ADA is but one piece of a larger and progressive policy framework of the political, economic, and social ecosystem needed to eliminate disability discrimination in educational, employment, health care, housing, governmental support programs, and in access to the built and digital environments. Changes in law and policy have been, and are, achieved incrementally and through the cumulative effects of advocacy, where discrimination is challenged and brought to the fore. Litigating disability rights has resulted in advances and retrenchment.

Nonetheless, to imagine the world without an ADA is to envision continued segregation, where human separation on the basis of functional difference alone is accepted. In this "It's a Wonderful Life" scenario, from the name of the classic film in which Clarence Odbody, AS2 (*Angel* Second Class) [24] helps George Bailey see what his world in Bedford Falls would have been like if he was never born and the town had become Pottersville,[24] disabled individuals and their families are unable to participate fully and have a community voice. There would

---

[23] Blanck, P. (2015). ADA at 25 and People with Cognitive Disabilities: From Voice to Action, *Inclusion* (forthcoming).

[24] IMBD (2015). Retrieved from http://www.imdb.com/title/tt0038650/.

be little tolerance for individual difference and accommodation of dissimilarity. Fundamental human liberties take on a skewed meaning, with equal participation only for some.

Unfortunately, the community of individuals with disabilities, and their families and supporters, know what it is like to live in Pottersville, the imagined city named after the villain in the film, Mr. Potter, a slumlord, who also uses a wheelchair. In the ADA and the UN Convention on the Rights of Persons with Disabilities, however, as former U.S. Attorney General Dick Thornburgh has said, "The world community has taken an important–and long overdue–step toward bringing people with disabilities all over the world into the mainstream of the human rights."[25]

Like General Thornburgh and many others in the disability community, I am optimistic but vigilant and determined about the future and the next twenty-five "A"s to come. And so, for the twenty-fifth "A," it is fitting that I turn back to *Abraham* Lincoln [25], for those immortal words he spoke at his first inaugural address on March 4 in 1861, one hundred and fifty-four years ago, about moral determination, yet compassion, to advance individual and collective rights. Lincoln (1861) spoke of us all:

> We are not enemies, but friends. We must not be enemies. Though passion may have strained, it must not break our bonds of affection. The mystic cords of memory...will swell... when again touched, as surely they will be, by the better angels of our nature.[26]

This line of study was supported in part by grants from the Administration on Community Living (ACL) and the National Institute on Disability,

---

[25] Thornburgh, D. (2012). *Respecting the Convention on the Rights of Persons with Disabilities, Testimony of Dick Thornburgh* before the Foreign Relations Committee of the U.S. Senate Hearing (July 12). Retrieved at http://www.foreign.senate.gov/ imo/media/doc/ Dick_Thornburgh_Testimony.pdf.

[26] Lincoln, A. *First Inaugural Address* (March 4, 1861). Retrieved from http://avalon. law.yale.edu/19th_century/lincoln1.asp.

David Ferleger, Esq.

Independent Living, and Rehabilitation Research (NIDILRR), in the U.S. Department of Health & Human Services, and the Office for Disability and Employment Policy (ODEP), in the U.S. Department of Labor. For information on this project and funding, see http://bbi.syr.edu.

Think About Where the Puck Is Going, and Go There

Michael Waterstone[1]

I frame my vision for the future of disability law with bits of wisdom from two sports greats.

Wayne Gretzky was perhaps the greatest hockey player of all time. When asked "What made you so good?," he would say, "I don't go where the puck is; I think about where the puck is going to be, and I go there."[2]

Contrast that with Yogi Berra who said, "It's tough to make predictions, especially about the future."[3] It's difficult to do.

The Americans with Disabilities Act was passed before I went to law school. For all intents and purposes, I've never known a world without it. It's important for all of us to acknowledge that in doing disability law work, we truly stand on the shoulders of giants who went before us as we think about moving ahead.

This topic makes me think about my late grandfather, an immigrant to this country, fleeing religious persecution. He loved this country, but it never really entered his consciousness to object too hard to things like Jewish quotas because he was just so happy that no one wanted to kill him for being Jewish. He thought that was the most amazing thing on the planet.

---

[1] Michael Waterstone is visiting professor of law at Northwestern Law School for the 2014-2015 academic year. He is also associate dean for research and academic centers and the J. Howard Ziemann Fellow and professor of law at Loyola Law School.

[2] https://www.goodreads.com/author/quotes/240132.Wayne_Gretzky.

[3] http://www.goodreads.com/quotes/261863-it-s-tough-to-make-predictions-especially-about-the-future.

My generation has the luxury of being greedy and continuing to fight for equality. It's like that with disability rights as well. In the next twenty-five years, we all have the real honor and benefit of thinking aggressively about notions of disability equality, imagining what a better future will look like. I talk about this from the vantage point of someone with the privilege and honor of teaching the next generation of advocates in this area.

As you may know, this new generation of advocates is coming. Some of them are law students with disabilities, some without, but they are coming. They want to give their talent, their idealism, their passion and energy to this movement. They are going to learn from us but also challenge us. The things that we have grown to accept drive them crazy.

I had an interesting conversation recently with my class. We were covering Title III of the ADA and the issue of whether the Internet is a place of public accommodation. These students can't understand a world where the Internet is not a place. These are students who shop online, see movies online. The whole concept of bricks and mortar is dated to them. Of course the Internet is a place. It's where they spend a lot of their time. They're different from previous generations.

I raise two hard issues here. The first is that most people don't think about the disability rights movement the way that we advocates and people with disabilities do. They don't think about disability rights the way we do. They don't think about it as a civil rights movement. Most of them don't think about it at all. When the Americans with Disabilities Act was passed, according to the Harris poll, most Americans were unaware of it.[4] That is very different than other civil rights movements.

This lack of awareness existed despite the fact that disability is the one minority group we can all join at any time. The country is currently engaged in a painful discussion about race and policing. Maybe nothing will happen as a result of that, but at least we're talking about it. We have to acknowledge that there's no parallel conversation going on about disability.

---

[4] "Poll: Most Support Integrating Disabled" (Jan. 9, 1982). http://articles. orlandosentinel.com/1992-01-09/news/9201070121_1_people-with-disabilities-disabilities-act-putting-disabled.

This lower political salience—that disability is something that people do not vote on, or ~~and~~ are not invested in—in some ways has been a real strength of our movement. It has enabled us to get legislation passed. It also has costs. In thinking about a twenty-five-year plan for disability rights, we need to find ways to get people to care about our issues.

The second hard issue is that judges don't see disability rights the way we do. We have a federal judiciary problem. Several years ago, I was fortunate enough to teach a training session on the Americans with Disabilities Amendments Act for federal magistrate judges. It became clear to me that many did not see this law as a civil rights statute. They see it as something that now is begrudgingly going to apply to a larger universe of people. "So I have a cousin with a backache, and now he needs this and that."

I have argued that the state of constitutional law contributes to the way in which judges see disability law. Constitutional law is quite negative on disability. I wish the Supreme Court's *Cleburne* decision required disability cases to be assessed using the standard of "rational basis scrutiny with teeth" rather than a weaker Equal Protection standard.[5] Other groups, such as the gay rights movement, have leveraged *Cleburne* in positive directions. In disability, however, *Cleburne* is always *Cleburne* equals rational basis equals the plaintiff with disability loses. This is despite the fact that Justice Marshall, who wrote the dissent in *Cleburne*, was right. The majority was wrong. The result in that case has had long-term effects. It limits what the ADA can do, and it is wrong.

What can we do on these hard issues? I have no easy answers, but I do offer up some suggestions on some longer term strategies. The idea is to balance the need to continue enforcing the laws that we have on a day-to-day basis but also to continue to think about how the laws are perceived by people.

There are state laws that still discriminate expressly on their face against individuals with disabilities, usually those with intellectual or psychosocial disabilities. These laws are rampant in family law and voting. My home state of California has a statute that requires

---

[5]   *City of Cleburne v. Cleburne Living Ctr.*, 473 U.S. 432 (1985).

reunification services for parents and children but denies them to parents with mental disabilities.[6] Based on these discriminatory laws, parents with disabilities face state proceedings to remove children from their care all too often. The Kentucky constitution still has a provision that bars idiots and insane persons from voting.[7] In targeting these laws that are still on the books, when we can, we should focus on state constitutions to challenge these laws, because sometimes state constitutions are more fertile grounds upon which to bring challenges. Connecticut, for example, has a state constitution that provides that no person shall be denied the equal protection of the law nor be subjected to discrimination because of, with a long list of categories, including physical disability in their constitutions.[8]

Here we need to look at our friends in the gay rights community who have utilized state constitutional litigation to move the needle on the federal constitution in terms of what is possible. Again, this is a twenty-five-year plan, not a five-year plan, but as a community we need to make some investment in that strategy.

The Constitution may not give us everything that the ADA does. But it is important to change constitutional understandings over time as they relate to disability. For my students and for me, it's simply unacceptable that the highest law of our land, which is our highest aspiration of who we want to be as a people, is so bad in our area. That needs to be on our twenty-five-year list of things to do.

When we talk about constitutional litigation, we need to acknowledge that that is not going to work for everyone that's covered by the ADA. Some people who are covered by the ADA realistically have no claim for any type of heightened scrutiny even under more liberal state laws. Constitutional litigation may work better for some groups than others. There are absolutely moments for cross-disability advocacy; there are limits to the use of the Constitution in such cross-disability work. We're at a point in the movement where we're unified enough to acknowledge differences and to face up to the fact that the ADA has worked better

---

6   Cal Wel & Inst Code § 361.5(c); Cal Fam Code § 7827.

7   Ky. Const. § 145(3).

8   Conn. Const. Amend. Art. XXI.

for some groups than for others. All movements have gone through this moment. It's okay to acknowledge that we can have cross-disability advocacy but also still at times pursue individual results and strategies.

On the Individuals with Disabilities Education Act, we need to constantly remember and push the idea that IDEA has its roots in *Brown v. Board of Education*. There is an argument that IDEA is constitutionally required, and we need to remember that that is what is behind that law. That statute, in fact, was preceded by federal court victories by students on constitutional grounds.

In terms of thinking about ways to get people to think about the issues that we do, and to care about them in the way that we do, certainly we want to continue doing what many advocates have been so brilliant at: finding cases that capture the imagination of people outside the movement. Family law presents fertile ground for that. I want to suggest something that I am not the first person to come up with Employment testing—and it doesn't even need to be brought in the legal sense. We all know that someone who uses a chair goes in and interviews, and someone without a chair interviews; both have the same qualifications. Who will get that job? Maybe the person without the chair.

I showed a video in my civil rights class from the late '80s in St. Louis, about a housing case, a television exposé, where a black person went in to rent an apartment. "Okay, thank you very much." A white person goes in. "Oh, yeah, of course, you get the apartment."[9] Caught it all on undercover cameras. That is powerful. You're able to capture what we all know happens and project that to people to show this is what is happening. That captures the imagination of people outside the movement.

Internationally, we have the Convention on the Rights of People with Disabilities (CRPD), which the United States has not ratified. I strongly believe that we should continue to push for ratification. I think it is the right thing for the United States and for the world. But we need to be very careful that ratification is not the endgame in and of itself.

---

[9]   *True Colors - Racial Discrimination in Everyday Life 2/2*, available at https://www. youtube.com/watch?v=gOS3BBmUxvs.

The way ratification is being pushed politically, it is just exporting our laws, rights, and values to the rest of the world, and if that helps us get it passed, great.

If it ends there, it is a huge missed opportunity. We need to continue to find ways to do what other countries are doing, which is to use the CRPD as a moment to reflect on our own laws and think about ways that we can improve what we do here and look for pressure points to pressure our government to do that. I reject the notion that we have nothing to learn from the rest of the world.

The last point I want to make comes back to students. We have the ability and the obligation that the next twenty-five years of law students learn from the people who came before them. We're at a moment where that can happen. One thing I would like to do to help that along, and there are ways now to reach students where they are with technology. I want to create a podcast series intended for law students taking disability courses. I want to talk to current advocates and lawyers about what they have done in the movement over recent decades, why they have done it, and what they think the next twenty-five years could be. We as law teachers can provide our students with the opportunity to listen, learn, and be inspired.

Like Wayne Gretzky, whom I quoted at the beginning of this essay, we need to think about where the puck is going to be, and go there.

What We May Yet Achieve

Robert Dinerstein[1]

In order to look ahead, I need to look back. No matter how good we think we are at predicting the future, it's really difficult to do well. Think about what life was like in 1990, and try to imagine what we would have said then about what the next twenty-five years to 2015 would have been like.

Let's remind ourselves of some of the things we now take for granted that didn't exist back in 1990 when the Americans with Disabilities Act was enacted, let alone in 1975 when the predecessor to the Individuals with Disabilities Education Act became law. For example, Facebook was not created until 2004.[2] Wikipedia wasn't created until 2001. Google was not created until 1998. A "googol" used to be a really big number with lots of zeros after it.[3] Cell phones weren't popular until 1997 and didn't get into the market until much after that. Smartphones were not really around until 1995. If you ever watch the old Seinfeld shows, you see the huge phones they used back then; it dates that show.

- Al Gore didn't invent the Internet until the 1990s.
- Email, which Millennials already consider passé, wasn't even around until the early 1990s.

---

[1] Robert Dinerstein is a professor of law and associate dean for Experiential Education at American University Washington College of Law.

[2] For this and other dates of societal occurrences between 1990-2015, I relied primarily on Wikipedia entries.

[3] http://www.google.com/about/company/history/. ("Google.com is registered as a domain on September 15[, 1997]. The name—a play on the word "googol," a mathematical term for the number represented by the numeral 1 followed by 100 zeros—reflects Larry and Sergey's mission to organize a seemingly infinite amount of information on the web.").

- Hybrid cars were not around until 1999.
- The Kindle was not available until 2007.
- Starbucks did not make its first profit outside of Seattle until the 1989-1990 period. Imagine a world without Starbucks! That was, for those of you who didn't live in Seattle, what the world was like in 1990.

In the process of thinking about the future, I also tried to look for inspiration in my own history, which for me is usually either about sports teams in the '60s or rock-'n-roll. I came up with that great song from the one-hit wonder Zager and Evans, "In the Year 2525," which made these predictions:

> In the year 2525, if man is still alive, if woman can survive, they may find.
>
> In the year 3535, ain't going to need to tell the truth, tell no lie. Everything you think, do, and say is in the pill you took today.
>
> In the year 4545, you ain't gonna need your teeth. Won't need your eyes. Won't find a thing to chew. Nobody will look at you.
>
> 5555, your legs got nothing to do. Some machine is doing that for you. [4]

You get the idea.

Luckily, I am not being asked to identify what might happen in the next 556 years, which is the math from when they wrote the song. More seriously, I am mindful of how wrong predictions can be. For example, in 2003 Justice O'Connor said, "We expect that twenty-five years from now, the use of racial preferences will no longer be necessary to further the interest approved today."[5] We can't know until 2028 whether her

---

[4] "In the Year 2525 (Exordium et Terminus)" is a 1969 hit song by the American pop-rock duo of Zager and Evans. It reached number one on the *Billboard Hot 100* for six weeks commencing July 12, 1969. http://www.songfacts.com/detail.php?id=1975. A video is at www.youtube.com/watch?v=izQB2-Kmiic.

[5] *Grutter v. Bollinger*, 539 U.S. 306, 343 (2003) (O'Connor, J.)

prediction will come true, but I would say from our history so far, it is not looking good.

We conduct this exercise of prediction in the context of a period rich with significant anniversaries of major civil rights and disability rights laws. Last year was the fiftieth anniversary of the 1964 Civil Rights Act. This year is the fiftieth anniversary of the Voting Rights Act and the fortieth anniversary of IDEA. In 2013, it was the fortieth anniversary of Section 504 of the Rehabilitation Act.[6] In thinking about the Voting Rights Act twenty-five years ago, would we have known that the Supreme Court would gut that act in the *Shelby County* case[7]? Some might have feared then that something like that could happen, but that is not the same as saying that such a result was predictable.

Thus, we have to be thoughtful—indeed, humble—about what we think will happen in the next twenty-five years and recognize that anything we say here is undoubtedly going to be wrong in some significant respects. We hope that if they are wrong, they are wrong in under-estimating the achievements in disability rights that many of us would wish to see.

So here are my predictions, issued with optimism and hoping for the best. I've taken the liberty to name some statutes after current colleagues in the disability rights movement. Although I provide some context for these citations below, the reader may feel free to Google them, though that is unnecessary to taking in the meaning of the predicted events.

In 2020, there was an interesting legislative development, one of the many times where people decided that an act's name needed to change. The Individuals with Disabilities Education Act was originally titled the Education for All Handicapped Children Act.[8] In 2020, Congress changed the name of the act to the Full and Meaningful Universal Educational Inclusion Act, which unfortunately doesn't have a really good acronym.

---

[6] *See* Laura Rothstein, *Forty Years of Disability Policy in Legal Education and the Legal Profession: What Has Changed and What Are the New Issues?*, 22 AU J GENDER, SOC POL'Y & THE LAW 519 (2014).

[7] *Shelby County, Alabama v. Holder*, 570 US __, 133 S. Ct. 2612 (2013).

[8] Pub. L. 94-142, 89 Stat. 773, *codified at* 20 USC 1401 et seq (1975).

Interestingly enough, that Act did two things that were important. One, it said that no longer will we be referring to the education of children with disabilities as special education. We will also no longer use the term "children with special needs" because we will just talk about people who need help, assistance, or whatever they want. That was a really nice thing that happened. Another provision of that Act was that the school districts were unable to argue going forward that they would do so much in inclusion in education if they only had the right training. That excuse has long been unavailing, and we felt good about statutory recognition of that in 2020.

In 2025, it was time for another legislative enactment. This was the Daniel Goldstein-Scott LaBarre Technology Accessibility Act.[9] That Act provided that no technology could be distributed in any situation anywhere in the country unless it was completely and fully accessible to people with any level of disability. Dan and Scott led a vibrant coalition of advocates and others to say that the time had come for this development, and they succeeded in making it happen.

In 2028, something else good happened as we think about the broader criminal justice system. The Supreme Court decided to ban the death penalty for everybody,[10] consequently bringing in under the ban people with severe mental illness and everyone else. That was during the presidential administration of George P. Bush.

In 2030, there was an important development in litigation. In litigation filed by David Ferleger,[11] the Supreme Court acknowledged

---

[9] Dan Goldstein is a partner in Brown, Goldstein & Levy, LLP, in Baltimore, MD. Scott LaBarre is principal in LaBarre Law Offices PC, in Denver, Colorado. Both have been very active in filing litigation and complaints with federal and state agencies requiring universities, businesses and other entities to make materials available in accessible formats.

[10] *See Glossip v. Gross*, 576 U.S. __, (Breyer, J., dissenting, slip op. at 1 ("But rather than try to patch up the death penalty's legal wounds one at a time, I would ask for full briefing on a more basic question: whether the death penalty violates the Constitution.").

[11] David Ferleger is an attorney with experience in the Supreme Court in disability cases. He has been a special master and court monitor for federal courts. *See* Ferleger, *The Constitutional Right to Community Services*, 26 Georgia State University Law Rev. 763 (2010).

there would be no more congregate institutions for people with intellectual disabilities.

In 2032, Senator Eve Hill introduced a bill, which was enacted into law, called the Gimme No More Shelter[12] law. The law got rid of the last sheltered workshop in existence,[13] which was well celebrated at the twenty-fifth tenBroek symposium sponsored by the National Federation of the Blind.

In 2035, during the President Chelsea Clinton Administration, the last state statute eliminating guardianship was passed in Virginia sponsored by State Senator Jenny Hatch.[14]

In 2037, the Laurence Paradis[15] Visitability Access Act was passed so that no new or even existing housing was allowed if it didn't provide for the ability of people in wheelchairs to visit others as they wanted to.

In 2038, Senator Lou Ann Blake introduced an amendment to the Help America Vote Act [16]called the Fully Accessible Voting Act, and it passed unanimously, which was really quite striking.

In 2039, Senator Peter Blanck[17] introduced the Anti-Acronym Amendments Act, the AAAA, which I would point out was inspired by his presentation at the 2015 tenBroek symposium because he was

---

[12] With apologies to the Rolling Stones.

[13] *See United States v. State of Rhode Island,* No. CA 14-175 (D RI, consent decree entered April 9, 2014), available at http://www.ada.gov/olmstead/documents/ ri-olmstead-statewide-agreement.pdf. Eve Hill was Deputy Assistant Attorney General in the Civil Rights Division when the consent decree was negotiated and entered.

[14] *See Ross v. Hatch,* No. CWF120000426P-03 (Va, Cir. Ct for Newport News, VA, August 2, 2013), *available at* http://www.supporteddecisionmaking.org/sites/ default/files/ross_hatch_trial_court_decision.pdf

[15] Laurence Paradis is the executive director and co-director of litigation for Disability Rights Advocates in Berkeley, California. He addressed the issue of visitability ordinances at the 2015 tenBroek symposium.

[16] Lou Ann Blake is, among other things, the Help America Vote Act project manager and tenBroek Disability Law Symposium coordinator for the National Federation of the Blind.

[17] Peter Blanck is university professor at Syracuse University and chairman of the Burton Blatt Institute.

so confused by the number of A's he had to come up with in his presentation.

In 2039, The New York Times published its last printed edition, and the headline on the front page that day was, "We admit we could have stopped using the term 'disabled' years ago, and we finally decided to do it."[18]

Also, in 2039, something occurred which was not a legislative or a court development. During the administration of President Kim Kardashian, the level of employment of people with disabilities finally reached the same level of people without disabilities of similar background, experience, and training. This was a major achievement of people at that time.

The Americans with Disabilities Act underwent its own name change in 2040, to focus on the concepts of universal design, equality, and the social model views of disability. The Americans with Disabilities Act was amended and would now be called the Right to Live and Thrive in the World Act of 2040.[19]

Oh, and the Chicago Cubs won the World Series in 2040, defeating the Texas Rangers four games to three.

---

[18] *See* email exchange between Robert Dinerstein and Philip B. Corbett, associate managing editor for standards, *The New York Times*, January 13, 2012 (on file with the author).

[19] *See* Jacobus tenBroek, *The Right to Live in the World: The Disabled in the Law of Torts*, 54 California L. Rev. 841 (1966),

Shaping Culture Change

Civil Rights Movements for People with Disabilities

Anita Silvers[1]

As I reflect on how working for civil rights generally, and for disabled people's rights specifically, has evolved over the past half century of my life, I see how the achievements, wisdom, and impressively determined character of Dr. Jacobus tenBroek inspired me and helped me stay on a steady–albeit challenging–course of disability advocacy during my fifty yearlong career as a college professor.

People with disabilities participated much more vigorously in the broader civil rights movement than historians have given us credit. During the post-World War II era when the great wave of civil rights activity gathered speed, disabled people contributed our skills to the movement to combat publically supported racial segregation. As historian Felicia Kornbluth has pointed out, Dr. tenBroek, who was blind, along with deaf historian Howard Graham, were approached by the National Association for the Advancement of Colored People (NAACP) to challenge the segregationist status quo. They did this by providing research and constitutional analysis about the Reconstruction Amendments to the United States Constitution in arguments the NAACP and the Justice Department made before the Supreme Court in the 1953 re-argument of *Brown v. Board of Education*.[2]

TenBroek and Graham claimed that a historically accurate reading, especially of the Fourteenth Amendment, was an activist and equalitarian one. The NAACP and Justice Department echoed their

[1] Anita Silvers is chair of the San Francisco State University Philosophy Department.

[2] Kornbluth, Felicia. *Turning Back the Clock: California Constitutionalists, Hearthstone Originalism, and Brown v. Board, California Legal History,* Vol. 7, 2012. 12/30/12. http://papers.ssrn.com/sol3/papers.cfm?abstract_id=2231521.

originalist, historicist approach when they argued successfully against segregation in public schools.[3]

The mid-twentieth century was an era in which our nation's capital, as well as many of the union's states, had laws preventing people of color from enjoying equitable access to public education and other public programs, as well as from being equitably served by businesses and other private organizations.[4] Although the Court at the time did not take up Dr. tenBroek's approach, sixty years later the Court may now be ready, at least occasionally, to venture a more equalitarian stance, one more inclusive of different kinds of minorities.

Even while working for other groups' civil rights, many of us found it hard to believe the desegregation movement eventually could also bring access to us. As an undergraduate badly crippled by childhood polio, I made my legs move through painful step after step for several hours on a picket line at the local Woolworths to support the right of African Americans to be served at lunch counters throughout the Woolworth national chain. Of course, I could not get up the steps to the Woolworth store my nondisabled college mates and I were picketing, nor were the high counter stools accessible to me.

Like many other disabled people in the Northern, Midwest, and Western states at that time, I was comfortable expressing outrage that an organization doing business in my local community excluded people of color at some of its other sites. But I feared opening up to reveal my distress, or even to be indignant, at that same organization's *de facto* excluding myself and other disabled people from lunching at Woolworth's counters all across the nation.

---

[3] *Id.*

[4] For example, due to racially segregated restaurants and hotels in Maryland and in the District of Columbia, the Kennedy administration had to deal with the perceptions of African diplomats that while both cold war protagonists – Russia and the United States. – were imperialist, the United States government had no concern about American racism targeting people of African descent. *See also* Vachon, Nicholas Murray. "The Junction: The Cold War, Civil Rights, and the African Diplomats of Maryland's Route 40". *Primary Source,* volume ii, issue ii. http://www.indiana.edu/~psource/PDF/Archive%20 Articles/Spring2012/2012%20-%20Spring%20-%208%20-%20Murray%20 Vachon,%20Nicholas.pdf#page=3&zoom=160,-11,367.

Later, in Baltimore, I joined my fellow Johns Hopkins graduate students in canvassing and getting out voters to defeat a ballot proposition that would have destroyed fair housing regulation. Sometimes I had to crawl up the steps to the doors of row houses to contact voters, but in those days access for individuals with mobility deficits was not even acknowledged as a goal in the fair housing debate.

Occasionally I allowed myself to think about the irony of pursuing access for other kinds of people when the desegregation movement seemed not to notice the barriers to equitable participation that prevailing social practice imposed on the liberty of disabled people like me. I feared dwelling on the troubling facts about the unfairness that pervaded disabled people's lives in our country. Civil rights seemed to be for nondisabled people only.

Dr. tenBroek had a much larger idea, and the courage and resilience to promote it. He saw that the values impelling the civil rights movement and bringing so many different kinds of people together were important for disabled people, because we too often suffer from such severe lack of access and equal treatment as to be segregated. In his enormously influential law review article "The Right to Live in the World,"[5] tenBroek pointed out that disabled people had no access to large areas of civil and commercial activity, as well as to the products that are earned by participation. Most importantly, the law does not treat disabled people equally. He argued that the integrationist policy established by the 1964 Civil Rights Act called for desegregation of disabled people as well as of racial minorities.

Most of us who had participated in actions to secure other people's civil rights had not supposed that in doing so we might be working for ourselves as well. I can't emphasize enough how liberating this understanding was in the mid-twentieth century, at least to people in disability categories that do not have a similar history of strong organizational representation, such as the National Federation of the Blind provides to the blind community.

---

[5] Jacobus tenBroek, *The Right To Live in the World: The Disabled in the Law of Torts.* California Law Review, Vol. 54, No. 2, May, 1966 *(841-919) https://nfb.org/images/nfb/publications/law/therighttoliveintheworldthedisabledinthelawoftorts.html.*

One day two students who were blind came into the philosophy department office and asked for me. They said they had heard there was a faculty member with a disability and had come to request I take on university officials on their behalf in regard to their ability to satisfy the university's general education requirements.

Unlike students who want to avoid completing requirements, these two students were complaining that they were being discriminated against because, against their own wishes, the university's math graduation requirement was being waived for them. From my own school days, this was familiar territory to me; in high school I had been labeled a risk in chemistry laboratory because in the previous year, stretching over a lab bench from a sitting position to execute a physics lab experiment that involved a lighted candle, I had singed my hair.

I dragged myself up three flights of stairs to confront the mathematics department chair.[6] I explained the easy solution to him—just let them stay enrolled in the course, and they would do the work. He protested that math instructors used the blackboard a great deal to demonstrate how problems ought to be solved. The department faculty had discussed the matter and decided the pedagogical problem loomed so large as to be stultifying; they didn't know how to teach freshman mathematics to blind students.

In fact, he said, to teach anything at all the instructor must write important information—to help the students take notes—on the blackboard. As it happens, I don't write on the blackboard when I teach because I can't reach high enough on it for students to see. In hindsight, I've been teaching with excellent student outcomes and ratings for nearly fifty years now and still am not able to write on the board.

My former students, many of whom have gone on to successful careers in the field, testify that they learned more than a little from me, but such future evidence did not yet exist. And I was feeling threatened by a presumption nondisabled people like the mathematics department chair so often and so erroneously make: thinking that the way they do things is the only way those things can be done.

---

[6] No San Francisco State University classroom or office buildings had elevators at that time.

I'm not sure what made the mathematics department chair relent. Possibly it was the novelty of the idea I then launched. As both students had completed four years of high school math with excellent grades (and were much more advanced in the discipline than most other students), I argued, why not ask them what they needed to learn math in the course? Surely *they* knew how they did it. Plus, after listening to sighted students complaining they had trouble with math and asking to be released from the requirement, there was the novelty of blind students whose high school grades showed they had no trouble with math and who desired to meet the mathematics requirement, instead of evading it.

Or else it was the novelty of facing an enraged female faculty member who apparently wasn't going to leave his office until he gave in. (Actually, I was trying to catch my breath for the laborious descent down three flights of stairs.)

Make no mistake. Although my action–rash for a not-yet-tenured assistant professor–was other-regarding in that I was defending other disabled people's right of access to a full public education, I also was acting to comfort myself. I was consoling my former self for all the opportunities I had been denied in the past based on my disability, and building confidence–or at least hope–that my future self, with support from a cross-disability movement, might be afforded wider access to the normal opportunity range.

I subsequently learned a lot about cross-disability advocacy from San Francisco State University's (SFSU) blind students. Fred Schroeder, now Dr. Frederic K. Schroeder of San Diego State University, was one of the students who guided me in this regard. After section 504 was added to the Rehabilitation Act in 1973, California public universities were for the most part very slow to comply. Disabled students across the state organized and came to Sacramento to testify to the legislature (successfully) about the burdens imposed on them just to obtain access to the locations and content of instruction.

Deaf students from the National Center on Deafness at California State University Northridge drove the only lift-equipped bus in the state university system north, picking up students using wheelchairs from other campuses. We caucused in the old Senator hotel across from the capitol. It was a privilege to participate as the deaf students and the blind students worked out how to engage in group discussions with each other. (The blind students relied on aural cues to know that one speaker had stopped and another could chime in without interrupting, while, for the deaf students, visual cues enabled them to integrate their contributions being conveyed by ASL interpreters into the vigorous strategy debate.) So far, no historian of the disability movement has researched the remarkable organizational effort of these students, nor recorded the leadership they continued to offer, in California and nationally, after they were awarded their degrees.

Parenthetically, I sometimes worry that today we rely too much on litigation, and therefore on courts, to apply policy, and too little on political action addressed to the hearts and minds of the public that, when all is done, influences courts in understanding the benefits of progressive disability policy.

Fast forward to this year, 2015, and another worry. We still have far to go, and it's unclear whether the post-ADA generation understands the importance of, and awareness needed for, cross-disability appreciation. We need to keep reminding ourselves that standing up for somebody else's rights–whether disabled people like ourselves, or disabled people very different from ourselves, or for nondisabled people–is reaching out to console and empower ourselves as well.

A few months ago, a troubling discussion surfaced on a Berkeley disability email list. A wheelchair user was complaining about having to roll over yellow metal plates with little bumps when approaching curb cuts in sidewalks, especially those that lead from commercial sites to parking lots. This individual wanted everybody to join a campaign to have the plates removed because crossing them makes for an uncomfortably bumpy wheelchair ride, and other list members jumped on this bandwagon.

This individual apparently had no idea why that metal plate is there. It marks the curb cut at the end of the side walk so blind pedestrians can feel it and refrain from walking head on into traffic. I was stunned; the campaigner apparently wasn't concerned about anything beyond personal comfort. The complainant did not understand why such metal plates appear.

This individual seemed concerned only with personal comfort and unaware of the history of struggle over installing curb cuts, even after legislation and subsequent regulation were in place. Initially after adoption of the revised Rehabilitation Act, cities' departments of public works were reluctant to comply with federal and state laws requiring path of travel access for wheelchair users. It was not unusual for them to delay by claiming that the curb cuts allowing wheelchair users to leave a sidewalk, cross the street, and get onto the sidewalk on the other side endangered blind people, who due to the curb cuts could not tell when they had left the sidewalk and thereupon become exposed to moving vehicles in the road.

The forbearance of the blind community, plus an agreement to mark the presence of curb cuts by inscribing a tactile warning in the concrete or installing a saliently tactile metal plate were needed to allay safety issues for blind people. I believe that honoring that agreement is an obligation for all disabled people whose lives are better due to the expansion of the civil rights movement to embrace disability rights, which includes almost every U.S. resident with a disability. Doing so is a stringent duty for wheelchair users who directly benefit from the blind community's generous cross-disability cooperation.

I hope, and trust, that soon I will be reassured to learn that disabled people are prepared to continue to work across disabilities, learning more about how other people with different disabilities than their own function and about other people's ways of life.

What if We Had a Civil Rights Movement, and Nobody Noticed?

Daniel Goldstein[1]

Recently, Marc Charmatz[2] and I were invited by the Journal of Race, Religion, Gender, and Class to give a talk. I thought, this will be nice, somebody is thinking about disability as part of diversity, which happens only occasionally as an afterthought. It is certainly not normally the case that disability and diversity are thought of together except among disability rights advocates.

My excitement was tempered somewhat by the fact that the invitation came from one of the editors who has been working for us as a paralegal for four years.

At that meeting, I was a little embarrassed to get up after Marc's recitation of *Access to the Courts: A Blueprint for Successful Litigation Under the Americans With Disabilities Act and the Rehabilitation Act*, on physical access for people with disabilities.[3] I just wasn't able to point to some landmark victory. I accepted that limitation, thinking that soon I would be writing this piece. This would be my chance to do a Daniel Goldstein version of "I have a dream," with Disney bluebirds singing as the sun rises. But then I started thinking about what I truly think about the next twenty-five years. I am going to be a real downer.

---

[1] Daniel Goldstein is a partner in Brown, Goldstein & Levy, LLP, in Baltimore, MD.

[2] Marc Charmatz is the longest serving staff member at the National Association of the Deaf.

[3] Marc Charmatz & Antoinette McRae, *Access to the Courts: A Blueprint for Successful Litigation Under the Americans With Disabilities Act and the Rehabilitation Act*, 3 U. Md. L.J. Race Relig. Gender & Class 333 (2003). Available at http://digitalcommons.law.umaryland.edu/rrgc/vol3/iss2/7.

Back when I was young, there used to be an expression, "What if they held a war and nobody came?" What if they had a civil rights movement and nobody noticed?

I don't think we've had our Selma, Alabama. Selma came into our home each night from Walter Cronkite, and whether we wanted to know or not know what was going on in Alabama and Mississippi in the 1960s, we were finding out because it was in our face to think about it and talk about it every night as we sat down to dinner.

I am not sure that the world has noticed that there is a disability rights movement yet. The law may be ahead of the culture change here, and it is really the implications of that on which I wish to focus, because I don't think in the end you can win without the culture change.

The core problem of disability rights is the misperception of persons with disabilities when they are visible, and the invisibility of persons with disabilities. The most common response when we sue a business or another entity of some kind over discrimination, is, "Oh, you know, we weren't thinking about people with disabilities when we. . . ." Fill in the blank: put in the curb cuts; designed the inaccessible software; didn't budget for ASL interpreters. Whatever. Like the Steve Martin Saturday Night Live routine: I forgot that bank robbery was a crime.[4]

The majority of people, when they encounter someone with a perceptible disability, think that it is only natural to believe that the disability limits opportunity. Recently, we had a blind student at a community college barred from taking any college class that had a lab, because of the belief that the student would be a fire hazard in the lab. We all know the key to the misperception problem: It's the word "amazing." For example, I saw this blind guy, and he scratched his ear without even knowing where his ear was. Wow, he's amazing! Consider when we do make the news. Ninety percent of the time it's what I call disability porn. This wonderful person who did something amazing and isn't that brave and heroic and so on.

The symbol of a person using a wheelchair in the bathrooms and parking spaces has been the most ubiquitous reminder to the oblivious

---

4   SNL Transcripts, Season 3: Episode 9, Jan. 21st, 1978. Retrieved from http:// snltranscripts.jt.org/77/77imono.phtml.

that they share the planet with persons with disabilities who also have rights.

We have to somehow solve these misperception and invisibility problems. A complicating factor is that the demographics of persons with disabilities will change, and with it, the perception of persons with disabilities. Genetic testing, amnio interventions, gene manipulation, and early detection of conditions will most certainly reduce the number of people with what are thought of as the more traditional disabilities such as spina bifida, dwarfism, certain kinds of deafness, autism, Down syndrome, etc. Replacement biotechnologies will also evolve and further mitigate conditions characterized by activity limitations if the implants and devices are affordable such as those for arthritic hips, shoulders, knees. I'm at the age now where I meet with an old friend and we start the "organ recital."

If the current research trajectory continues, smart technologies will radically reduce the impact of other limitations such as vision loss. Chemical advances will generate new drugs for scores of physical and mental conditions that impair function and cognition.

These developments will strengthen the medical narrative that is so antithetical to rights. I am not saying these developments are bad. I am saying these developments will strengthen the narrative that disability is a medical issue. What happens if there are only 20 percent as many blind children in the school system and we have all this technology? Are we really going to be able to insist on Braille literacy and succeed in getting people to understand why Braille is so important and has to be provided?

What happens if the co-occurrence of disability and age increases? This is possible, although a lot of money is going to research around the growing aged population. It will strengthen a perception of disability as associated with a general lessening of capabilities because many older people are limited in their ability to learn new adaptive techniques that would mitigate the impact of the disability. The association of age and disability will strengthen the perception of disability as extremely limiting. If you see that Great Aunt Josie can't do X, Y, Z anymore because of a particular disability, you're going to think that is characteristic of the disability rather than characteristic of Great Aunt Josie.

If the general public sees few of us in job positions carrying on a normal life and sees more of us as Great Aunt Josie, we're going to have image problems.

I do think there will be areas in which we will see an increase in disabilities. I predict, sadly, that as income inequality continues, we're going to see a closer and closer intimacy between poverty and disability. We may well see increases in PTSD, diabetes, respiratory conditions, and behavioral and emotional disabilities in our poor neighborhoods, because the triggers for those disabilities are right there in poverty.

Just as there are many who believe that the poor are poor as a matter of personal failure, that belief can extend to things like obesity and diabetes. My partner Andrew Levy told me that at Bon Secours Hospital in Baltimore, which serves a poor population, the number one most frequent surgical procedure is amputation related to diabetes.[5]

It is likely we are going to see an increase in the incidence of disability in the developing world, or at least less of a decrease compared to the demographics in the United States and Europe. The face of disability may be that of Sierra Leone or Haiti, very much strengthening the pity narratives that are so antithetical to rights.

All of which is to say that if we look at disability rights as purely a matter of law, I think we are in big trouble. We have to focus very hard on communicating to the world who we are and what it means to be who we are, what it means to be disabled. This in huge part depends on what people believe that word means, and that meaning is going to change with or without us. It is not too soon to create a concerted effort to learn how we can guide the cultural conversation and make that part of what we think about as we do our work.

---

[5] Andrew Levy currently serves as co-host and occasional guest host of FOX News Channel's (FNC) *Red Eye with Greg Gutfeld* (weeknights 3-4AM/ET). He joined the network in 2007. See http://www.foxnews.com/on-air/personalities/andy-levy/bio/#s=h-l.

Culture Change:
A Foundation to Policy Change

Ari Ne'eman[1]

I would like to begin with an anecdote from the birth of the ADA. At the signing ceremony for the Americans with Disabilities Act, Pat Wright and Senator Ted Kennedy sat next to each other, and they had a very interesting exchange. They had both played an absolutely critical role in the passage of this legislation. They had both been involved from the very beginning to the very end. As President Bush, the first President Bush, reached to sign the seminal civil rights document for people with disabilities, Senator Kennedy leaned over to Pat and said, "Pat, what if he reads it first?"

I've always loved that story because I think it captures the fact that the disability rights movement is somewhat unique in the annals of civil rights movements in that very frequently our policy, and our legal and our legislative victories in fact, come well before the types of cultural or social change that in other movements have preceded law or policy or litigation.

That has had a very significant impact on how our movement has operated and the degree to which the law and policy and litigation battles that we have won has been enforced.

The ADA itself has already required legislative efforts to strengthen it. In the aftermath of the passage of the ADA (despite the clear intent of advocates in Congress to encompass a broad definition of disability, to focus the conversation on discrimination rather than an "Are they

---

[1] Ari Ne'eman is the president and co-founder of the Autistic Self Advocacy Network.

or aren't they?" approach to whether or not people are disabled) courts adopted an overly narrow definition of disability, requiring Congress and the advocacy community to pass the ADA Amendments Act of 2008.

The reason for narrow judicial approach was not because the ADA was inexpertly drafted. I'm sure that any one of the dozens and hundreds of people who claim to be the author of the ADA would attest that they did it right the first time.

The reason was that our culture had not yet, and in many ways still has not yet, adjusted to the idea that disability is a broad social and cultural identity and does not equate to whatever one has seen in the movies or whatever one sees on television or reads in some small collection of diagnoses. There is a prevalent view that this population cannot be trusted to succeed or to be included or to have a quality opportunity to enjoy our own rights.

Because we have not undertaken the necessary cultural and social change to safeguard and advance our policy victories, we often find ourselves in the position of playing catch-up, even on questions of law that we thought were long settled.

Much of my work has to do with conversations on Medicaid finance, long-term services and supports. In particular, getting people with disabilities out of segregated and restricted settings like institutions, sheltered workshops, segregated day activity centers, and other similar environments, and instead encouraging states to meet their obligations under the Americans with Disabilities Act and the *Olmstead* decision and serve people within the most integrated setting. One of the most concerning trends that we have seen in recent years is that as states have faced growing pressure both from the Medicaid Money Follows the Person program and the Community First Choice option, and the exemplary homestead enforcement over the last several years, we have seen efforts by states and providers, rather than shift how they are providing services to people, to offering settings which are clearly institutions rebranded as community based.

A classic example of this occurred several years ago. The state of Missouri decided it would close the Nevada Habilitation Center. (It is called the Nevada Habilitation Center. It's in Missouri.) Missouri planned to take the residents of that institution and place them in a series of large group homes on the grounds of the old institution, staffed by the same people who worked in the old institution, around which Missouri would place a fence and refer to it all as a "gated community." For this, Missouri desired federal community waiver funding. The federal government in 2011, after outcry from the advocacy community, took steps to indicate that this was not an acceptable use of Home and Community Based Waiver funding.

We see things of this nature all the time. There is a growing and concerning movement in this country, driven by some in the parent community and the provider community, to set up these types of segregated housing complexes, villages, and farmsteads. They go by everything from autism farms to gated communities to dude ranches for Down's syndrome.

What we have to remember is that the people who are driving this rebranding and essentially re-institutionalization have in many ways forgotten the legacy of Willowbrook. They have internalized the idea that the old institutions were bad because they were staffed by villains who decided to hurt people on a daily basis. In reality, we know that isn't true. Many of the staff of the old institutional settings became some of the strongest advocates for deinstitutionalization in the developmental disability and mental health deinstitutionalization movements, because they saw the horrors of institutional settings.

In reality, we know that particularly for people with the most significant and complex needs, there is something inherently, structurally problematic about saying to people that in order to receive services, you need to live with fifty, sixty, or one hundred of your nearest and dearest strangers with whom you happen to share a diagnosis. Because we have not made the cultural progress necessary to safeguard our legal victory in *Olmstead*, we see this continue to come back.

In response to the Missouri situation and a wide variety of other similar situations, the federal government realized that there was still a long way to go in deinstitutionalization. We needed to focus not only on closing large state facilities, but we have to recognize that too often we had taken people out of large settings where somebody else controlled every aspect of their daily lives and put them into small settings where somebody else controlled every aspect of their daily lives.

In short, the size and congregate nature of the setting mattered in determining whether or not something is institutional in nature. Also, the rights and opportunities available to people with disabilities being served even in small settings matter in determining whether or not something is institutional in nature. *Olmstead*, as an idea, and community integration, as a value, have relevance not only to where people live or work or receive services, but also to the way in which those services are provided. If you are forty-five years old and the person who runs your group home tells you when your bedtime is, you are living in an environment that is institutional in nature. If somebody else is setting the rules that define your life in a way that would not be occurring for somebody who did not have support needs, that implies that you are in an environment that is institutional in nature.

Last year, the federal government issued a new set of regulations that Autistic Self Advocacy Network and many others in the advocacy community are watching very closely. These rules articulated a higher standard for what constitutes home and community based services. The rules are relevant both to funding and to where and in what ways those services are provided. On the latter, people receiving home and community based services under these rules have rights to privacy, to choice, to autonomy, and to a choice of settings for all available options, including nondisability specific options. Provider owned settings, where a service provider is also a landlord, are recognized as posing a particular risk to the individual. The rule therefore provides, for example, a prohibition on individuals being forced into regimented meal and sleep schedules, a right to receive visitors in one's own home, and a right to decorate one's home.

The fact that these types of rights need to be articulated in Medicaid rules seems to suggest that we still have a long way to go to achieve the social and cultural change necessary to assure people with disabilities the recognition, rights, and opportunities which the nondisabled population takes for granted.

When we talk about the future of the ADA, and when we talk about the future of the disability advocacy movement, we need to be thinking about the next stage in policy victories. As I have said, underlying social and cultural change is essential to making progress sustainable. One approach in this direction is the annual leadership academies convened by the Autistic Self Advocacy Network. In three locations across the country, we bring emerging disabled leaders from across the country together for a week of advocacy training.

At these trainings, what amazes and inspires me about this next generation of young people is the degree to which many of them have had the opportunity to be immersed in the ideas of the disability rights movement, the self-advocacy movement and of community integration from a very young age. They did not have to find disability community only in adulthood. For a growing percentage of our own community, disability culture and disability rights are something that they are growing up with from day one.

If we are to secure the kinds of social, cultural, and other forms of change necessary to make our political and legal victories sustainable, making disabled individuals aware of disability culture and disability rights from day one represents a critical aspect of what our larger strategy must be. If we do not ourselves understand that we as a community have rights and recourse, that the problems of disability are an obligation of society to remedy; then we will have a very difficult time in making that understood to others. If we can build the next generation of disability advocates with a mindset that presumes that they are people and that as people they have certain rights that they should be able to enforce, we will have a valuable grounding, a valuable first step, toward convincing the larger culture of that same thing.

Shaping the Judiciary

Access to the Courts:
A Model Future, Achieved Today

Richard Brown[1]

I am retiring from my position as chief judge of the Wisconsin Court of Appeals in August of this year. I was elected to the bench in 1978 and took office on August 1, 1978, when I was thirty-three years old. On the date of my retirement, I will have served for thirty-seven years. It is time to go.

I'll tell you how I came to this conclusion. I went to the annual Wisconsin Judicial Conference last year. This occurs once a year and almost all of the judges in Wisconsin attend. There were a lot of new faces there. Younger faces. I recalled that, in 1978, when I went to my first conference, I was the youngest judge in Wisconsin. I didn't know a soul at that conference. Back then, in 1978, the attendees were all a bunch of cranky, old white men. I don't think there was one black judge, and if I recall correctly, only one woman.

Five years later, I knew every judge at the conference, all 251 judges. I knew them all.

When I went to the conference last year and saw all these young people, I didn't know anybody but the retired judges who were on reserve status. That's when I knew it was time to retire.

But I am not retiring from involvement in disability issues. I always feel so alive being around people involved in this field because of their passion and dedication. Together, we are actually changing the way this country works, changing how we are perceived by society and by the courts. It is personally so uplifting to be a part of this.

---

[1] Hon. Richard S. Brown is chief judge of the Wisconsin Court of Appeals.

I am going to talk about the Wisconsin experience as it relates to enabling the participation of people with disabilities in legal proceedings. I am from Wisconsin and therefore have firsthand knowledge of it. But more importantly, I want to relate to you how Wisconsin's courts have moved forward on accessibility issues while "horror stories" are recounted in some other states. I hope that we can use the Wisconsin experience as kind of a model for state court systems to follow when seeking to enable the participation of people with disabilities in court-related matters.

No doubt, most of you have read about the polarization evident in our Wisconsin supreme court and the personal animosities that have been made public. Despite this, I can tell you that whatever you may be reading in the newspapers has had no effect on how our court system is responding to the needs of persons with disabilities.

Now, I mentioned earlier the "horror stories" out there where courts-systems are either ignorant of their responsibilities under Title II of the ADA or are fully cognizant of their duties but intentionally choose to ignore them. But we have done something in Wisconsin, which has worked. It actually began in Reno, Nevada, in 1991. A national conference was convened to discuss court-related needs of the elderly and people with disabilities. It consisted of four daylong working sessions. There were a lot of discussions and give-and-take. From these discussions, recommendations were made on how to proceed. The Reno conference resulted in a 270-page report entitled "Blueprint for the Future," which included the recommendations that emerged from the conference. Each recommendation was accompanied by issue summaries and policy papers discussing the substance of the particular recommendations. The "Blueprint" also listed selected state action plans.

Five of us attended from Wisconsin. Before returning home, the five of us resolved to ask the chief justice to form a committee to pursue a state action plan for Wisconsin. The chief justice, to our delight, convened a thirty-member interdisciplinary committee to study and make recommendations to ensure that the elderly and people with disabilities have equal access to the state's court system. The committee applied for and was approved for a grant from the State Justice Institute for a fifteen-month term, from January 1, 1993 to March 31, 1994. The grant provided for the hiring of a full-time project coordinator.

The goals of the committee were as follows: (1) survey the Wisconsin courts to assess current accessibility; (2) conduct public hearings; (3) make contact with other state court systems; (4) conduct outreach to Wisconsin advocacy groups and networks for the elderly and people with various disabilities; and (5) submit a written report by the end of March 1994 setting forth its recommendations for improving access to the judicial system for people with disabilities.

It is important to remember that the ADA had just become effective when the committee first met. There was no guidance from court decisions on the ADA. The committee was literally starting from scratch. Yet the committee, meeting twice a month, submitted its report in a timely manner.

I have been on several task forces where written reports and recommendations were made, only to collect dust on some shelf. When I was asked to speak at this 2015 conference on the topic of how to enable the participation of people with disabilities in legal proceedings, I dug out my twenty-one year old copy of our report and went through it.[2] When I finished reading it, I was amazed to discover that much of what had been recommended by the committee was implemented by our court system. That is when I realized that the report was not something collecting dust somewhere but was actually a good starting point for a model by which courts still having problems with accessibility issues could use. So, the report and its aftermath are what I want to discuss here.

The report is 116 pages long, not including the appendices. So, I cannot cover all of it. But I can give you a picture. We divided our committee into several subgroups, as follows: (1) physical access; (2) communications access; (3) access to the jury process; (4) training recommendations; and (5) cost issues. We had public hearings covering all of these subjects. And, in our report, each committee made specific

---

2   *Access: Final Report of the Wisconsin Supreme Court Interdisciplinary Committee on Court-Related Needs of the Elderly and People with Disabilities, 1994.*

recommendations and the rationale for them. Finally, and importantly, the committee as a whole provided general recommendations.

With the benefit of hindsight in 2015, here are a few recommendations that have passed the test of time and which are still worth discussing today. The first thing that stood out to me in reading the report was the committee's take on the ADA rule that every government should have an ADA coordinator. The committee knew even then that there are ADA coordinators and then there are real ADA coordinators. We knew, for instance, that if a county hired an ADA coordinator, that coordinator would not be court specific, but would be more like a generalist—such as working on access to the public library or transportation issues in getting citizens with disabilities to a government event. These ADA coordinators would not be trained by the courts and would likely have little understanding of the needs of the court system. So, our committee recommended that there be an ADA coordinator in each county courthouse and that the courts train these coordinators.

We also were cognizant of the fact that the judges run the courts. A lot of you who practice litigation know this all too well. Judges run their own court, and they are not going to let anybody tell them otherwise. They set the calendar, they set the tone and demeanor of the courtroom, and they are the ones that delegate duties and responsibilities to the staff. So, in our mind, if we were going to have effective ADA coordinators, we had to get our judges to buy in. To that end, we had numerous programs at our state judicial education conferences designed to provide an understanding of the ADA, the need to be cognizant of accessibility issues, and the necessity of having someone on the staff ready to resolve accessibility issues.

The result has exceeded expectations. I can tell you in 2015 that all of the judges in our state are empathetic about accessibility issues. The printed forms and notices have a box asking people to contact the ADA coordinator if they have a disability and need an accommodation. That is an "early warning" system. Judges then are made aware that there is an accessibility issue that must be resolved before the judicial proceeding takes place. The judge then interacts with the county court ADA coordinator. But it doesn't necessarily stop there. There is a state ADA coordinator who is housed in the Court Management and Court Operations division of our court system in Madison, our state capitol.

She is the "go to" person that the judge or county ADA coordinator can depend upon if needed. She is often turned to for guidance on how to resolve an accommodation issue if it cannot be easily handled locally. That state coordinator's main job is to find the accommodations that the county needs. The state coordinator knows who to call. If the accessibility issue involves a piece of equipment, the state coordinator can get it. If a person needs C.A.R.T.,[3] and there isn't one available in the county where the request has been made, the state coordinator can get one. The same thing is done if a person needs a sign language interpreter.

If you really want to make a change in your state system, a good ADA coordinator program is the place to start. If you really want to make a change, go to the people who make the ultimate decisions—such as the chief justice—or someone with similar powers. I suggest that each state do what we did in Wisconsin: form an interdisciplinary committee to make specific recommendations. The first step is to get the trial judges to buy in. The second step is for the judges to designate an ADA coordinator for their jurisdiction. And the third step is to get a state ADA coordinator who can actually coordinate things.

After reading the *Final Report on Access* and re-familiarizing myself with it, I contacted our state ADA coordinator and went through, with her, the various issues that the interdisciplinary committee had dealt with—physical access, communication, access to the jury process, training, and costs. She said that, with respect to physical access, she has not had a building facility complaint in four years. That's largely because accessibility awareness came along at the right moment for us in Wisconsin—a bit of luck—because, at that time, many of Wisconsin's counties were already planning new or remodeled courthouses. It was comparatively easy, therefore, to build ADA accessibility into these plans. Now, you walk into a new courthouse in Wisconsin and you see handrails, Braille, wide hallways for wheelchair users to navigate, courtrooms that are easy to get into and out of, elevators—all kinds of things that weren't contemplated when the old courthouses were built and, frankly, were not part of the discussion when planning the

---

[3]   C.A.R.T. is a Communication Access Real-time Translation device for individuals who are deaf or hard of hearing.

new or remodeled courthouses until the interdisciplinary committee got involved. I'll give you an example of a remodeled courthouse. In several of our old courthouses, we had courtrooms with marble floors, ceilings 100 feet high, dark paneled walls, and lights that gave off a dark tone. The remodeled courtroom had a carpeted floor, a lowered ceiling, soundproof walls with brighter colors, and excellent lighting. This made the courtroom much more accessible to the hard of hearing and deaf. Certainly, the new courtroom was not as majestic and beautiful as it used to be, but it was much more functional.

I already referred to the early warning system. I can't emphasize enough how important this was. Before this, nobody knew ahead of time if there was going to be an accessibility issue. Nobody knew how to get in touch with the person with a disability. Now, it's on every form. Someone wants to make a small claims complaint? It's on the complaint form. You're answering the complaint? It's on that form. You have a deposition? It's on the notice form. In that form, the person with a disability is urged to get in touch with the court within a certain time frame so that any accommodation issue can be addressed.

I have mentioned the training of judges and staff. Despite the intensive training at judicial conferences and seminars, some judges did not buy in at first. They would not act on providing an accommodation. Or they would not have a hearing to determine whether the requesting person needed an accommodation if they suspected that the person did not need one. In fact, we had a judge who steadfastly refused to have a hearing on an accommodation request until the date of the trial or hearing. We had another judge who, based on prior experience with the litigant, disbelieved the litigant's request for an accommodation and decided not to have a hearing at all. As a result of these instances, an appellate opinion mandated that hearings take place before the controversy is tried if there is an accommodation issue and the court is not convinced that an accommodation is necessary or is not convinced that the *requested* accommodation is necessary and an alternative accommodation would suffice. Now, in Wisconsin, judges must have a hearing if there is a question about an accommodation, and it must be well before the trial or hearing takes place.

Of course, for most of our judges, it never comes to that. If a request for an accommodation comes in, the court is proactive in getting that accommodation without any need for a hearing in the first instance.

Another interesting fact came out of my discussion with the state ADA coordinator. We now have, in every courthouse in seventy-two counties, at least one C.A.R.T. reporter. In 1994, there were ten in the whole state. Now there's one in every county. This, I believe, is an outgrowth of a recommendation of our committee that the county buy the real-time equipment rather than the reporter having to buy it. We also recommended that the state or the counties pay for the real-time training. And that is exactly what happened. Now, we can see the results. It used to be that reporters shied away from real time. Now, it is the rule rather than the exception.

We now have large print production services as recommended by the committee. We have personal readers if requested. We have a tremendous sign language interpreter program filled with people who have been deemed qualified by the Registry of Interpreters for the Deaf. These people know what they're doing. I will wager that, in 1994, we had maybe two in the whole state.

And here is something else we have done. There are people who, because of mental disability, have an issue with being in a place like a courtroom where they are way too anxious and cannot function well. They prefer to be in a different place when being asked questions under oath by a lawyer. The movement has been to allow this accommodation despite objections from the bar—who want the witness in the courtroom. But, slowly, the bar is learning to give-and-take because each situation is different. On an individual case-by-case basis, the judge can get the parties together and agree to use video where a large screen is in front of the person with the disability and that person can see the judge on that screen when the oath is being given. So, when the oath is made, it means something. There is a certain air of respect and confidence in the system. We are beginning to see more and more the remote use of video, which allows people to participate even though they are not in the courtroom.

Then, there is the jury process. Back in 1994, the main question was, where does the ADA stop? Does it stop at the courthouse steps? At the courtroom door? Or, some other place. Many people on the committee, a majority, believed that the ADA stopped at the steps. We were wrong then. We were so focused on the brick and mortar courthouse that we didn't consider the connection from the outside. That's all changed now. Now, there is at least serious discussion about providing transportation services for jurors who have a disability that creates a problem for getting to the courthouse. I don't know if this is statewide, but I do hear of some counties where this has been done. This would be of great help to jurors with transportation issues due to inaccessibility.

We have a jury handbook that discusses access. The person who is going to be called for jury duty receives the handbook a month or two in advance, so each prospective juror knows he or she can get an accommodation. All she or he has to do is call a number.

We've changed the statutes. The statutes used to call for things like having jurors raise their right hands to take the oath. Well, some people can't raise their hands. So, we had that language taken out.

We now ensure that wheelchair users are not segregated. Building improvements have made this possible to a large extent.

Now, I want to come to something that was of great interest to me when I was on the committee in 1994 and remains so today. Costs. There is the persistent claim that providing the accommodation is too costly; county boards saying they don't have the money to provide an accommodation; single practitioners saying that if they have to pay for a sign language interpreter, for instance, that will eat up any profit. Undue burden has been a big issue. It was in 1994 and still is now.

What we tell lawyers is that it is inappropriate to compare the cost of an auxiliary service with the payment received from the client. We say that you can't compare it with whether you are going to make a profit on that particular case. The proper comparison is between the cost of the interpreter and the resources or overhead you have in your office over the calendar or fiscal year. That changes the equation.

Now, many lawyers don't like this because they see things in black and white—get a case, get a fee, and measure it against the costs of the case. But that isn't the way the ADA law works. Interestingly, the Colorado Bar Association has tackled this issue by creating a fund from which lawyers can receive payment for costs associated with providing services to people with disabilities. This is a wonderful thing, and I wish all bar associations did this. When I get back to Wisconsin, I am going to urge our bar to do it. You should too.

There is also an IRS tax incentive for public accommodations that incur expenses for access. This is called the Disabled Access Credit. It includes reasonable amounts paid or incurred and you get 50 percent of the eligible expenses that exceed $250 but not more than $10,500.

Sometimes, the government is willing to provide the accommodations, but the sticking point comes when one arm of government wants another arm of government to take it out of its budget. For example, say that a criminal defendant is meeting with a state public defender in the defenders office to get ready for a trial. Who pays for the accommodation? The state public defender may argue that the court should bear the cost because the meeting is in connection with a court proceeding. But the pattern developing is one of physical presence. If the accommodation is needed at the police station, the police pay out of the police budget. If it is in the state public defender's office, it is the defender who pays. If it is in the courthouse, it is the court that pays. That is how it has worked in Wisconsin anyway.

How does it look for the future? I can't prognosticate twenty-five years ahead, but I can tell you this. I told you at the beginning of my discussion, and I am telling you now. If you can get a group together to seek funding for an interdisciplinary committee that provides a blueprint for the state, and if you have all the stakeholders involved, and if you get the judges to buy in due to training sessions, then my prediction is that the horror stories that occur in your state might dissipate.

Shaping the Issues

The United States Department of Justice: Unprecedented Opportunities

Vanita Gupta[1]

We at the United States Department of Justice, Civil Rights Division– and I in particular–am proud to be a partner in the ongoing fight for civil rights for people with disabilities. The Division is energized to do disability rights work, and it is one of my highest priorities.

This year, we will celebrate the twenty-fifth anniversary of the Americans with Disabilities Act (ADA) and the fortieth anniversary of the Individuals with Disabilities Education Act (IDEA). We've made a lot of progress since then. But, as President Obama once said, "As long as we as a people still too easily succumb to casual discrimination or fear of the unfamiliar, we've still got more work to do."

Disability discrimination is alive and well in this world. We at the Civil Rights Division take on flat-out discrimination every day of the week. We also take on more subtle forms of discrimination that have effects just as devastating as the more obvious forms of discrimination. Regardless of the form disability discrimination takes, it damages not just those it directly affects, but our entire community. As a community, we cannot afford not to include people with disabilities in every aspect of life.

Some of the obvious examples of discrimination that we still confront include:

---

[1] Vanita Gupta is principal deputy assistant attorney general and acting assistant attorney general for the Civil Rights Division at the United States Department of Justice.

- Banks like Wells Fargo refusing to accept relay calls from deaf customers. The Justice Department's settlement required Wells Fargo bank to adopt effective communication and nondiscrimination policies and provide $16 million in monetary relief for customers nationwide.[2]
- We recently reached a settlement with the Law School Admission Council to reform its testing accommodation policies and stop "flagging" LSAT scores of test-takers with disabilities who get the accommodation of extra time. That settlement requires nearly $8 million in monetary relief as well as a $55,000 civil penalty.[3]
- We settled with the Louisiana Bar to stop asking intrusive and unnecessary mental health questions on its bar application and to stop imposing conditional admission requirements on people with mental health conditions just because of their disabilities.[4]
- Our Barrier-Free Health Care Initiative continues to find doctors, hospitals, and other healthcare facilities that discriminate against people with disabilities—whether refusing to provide sign language interpreters, not offering accessible facilities, or denying service to people with HIV. We have reached seven agreements with healthcare facilities this year to address those issues.[5]

Some more subtle examples of discrimination happen in some of the most important areas of life—parenting, the Internet, education, criminal justice, community living, and employment.

Parenting

Parenting has frequently been found by courts to be a fundamental right. Yet a report by the National Council on Disability recently noted

---

[2] Disability Rights online News, *Wells Fargo Agrees to Comprehensive Settlement of ADA Issues*, July 2011.

[3] http://www.ada.gov/lsac_consentdecree.htm

[4] The United States' Investigation of the Louisiana Attorney Licensure System Pursuant to the Americans with Disabilities Act (DJ No. 204-32M-60, 204-32-88-204-32-89)

[5] U.S. Attorney Program for ADA Enforcement, Barrier-Free Health Care Initiative, http://www.imiaweb.org/uploads/docs/DOJADA.pdf.

significant overrepresentation of parents with disabilities in state child welfare systems and concluded that much of that overrepresentation was due to bias. We recently saw just such bias in the Massachusetts Department of Children and Families' (DCF) decision to remove a two-day old infant from her mother who has an intellectual disability.[6]

Although DCF's policies support reunification and DCF had a number of services available to help with reunification, DCF didn't offer that family all the services it offered other families, didn't accept that the child's grandparents wanted to take guardianship and help raise the child with their daughter in their home, didn't consider that the mother was taking parenting classes and pursuing her high school diploma, and didn't appear to consider it a serious possibility that the child could ever be returned to her mother—just because the mother had an intellectual disability.[7] DCF finally moved to terminate the mother's parental rights.

We investigated and, together with the Department of Health and Human Services, found that DCF was violating the ADA in discriminating against the mother because of her disability. We demanded they provide the reunification services available to all other parents, as well as any services needed as reasonable modifications and compensatory damages.

After over two years of separation, the grandmother was awarded guardianship, and the child was returned to her family. Our discussions with the state are continuing.

Internet

The growing reliance on the Internet and other technologies for access to everything from groceries to education to employment has great potential to be an equalizer for people with disabilities—but only

---

[6] Investigation of the Massachusetts Department of Children and Families by the United States Departments of Justice and Health and Human Services Pursuant to the Americans with Disabilities Act and the Rehabilitation Act (DJ No. 204-36-216 and HHS No. 14-182176).

[7] *Id.* at 5.

if those technologies are built accessibly. The National Federation of the Blind, Disability Rights Advocates, Lainey Feingold, the National Association of the Deaf and others have been leaders in demanding accessibility of websites and other technologies from the beginning, and we are proud to have joined in that work.

We're addressing accessibility of technology in settlements with colleges like Louisiana Tech, which will now only buy instructional technology that's accessible, and with public accommodations like Peapod online grocery delivery service, which will make its website accessible.

We've also recently included reviews of state and local governments' websites in our Project Civic Access compliance review programs, requiring jurisdictions like Nueces County, Texas, to make their websites compliant with the Web Content Accessibility Guidelines 2.0.

And, in compliance reviews of public entities' hiring practices, we've made them stop asking pre-employment questions about disability in their online job applications and required them to make those online applications compliant with WCAG 2.0.

Education

We recently reached agreement with Quinnipiac University for placing a student on mandatory medical leave after she considered suicide, without considering other ways of accommodating her education while she sought treatment, such as allowing her to take classes–in person or online–and live off campus.

Criminal Justice

We're also transforming how police departments and prisons deal with people with disabilities. There has been a lot in the news lately about police response to young black men, racial profiling, and excessive force. We do those cases. But what you may have heard less about is police response to people with mental illness and other disabilities. It has been reported that half the shootings by police each year are of people with disabilities.[8]

We have taken on this issue in our ADA enforcement because too often we've found police coming to help someone with mental illness, but the person is in crisis and can't follow directions. Too often, police officers do not have the training to respond to people with mental illness. As a result, officers called to help someone may end up injuring or killing the person because of the tragic confluence of circumstances. Last year we reached an agreement with the Portland, Oregon, Police Bureau to reform its response to people with mental illness.

We're seeing the results already. According to the local Portland paper, police officer Zachary DeLong was called to a burglary report.[9] He found a man on the ledge of a hotel five stories up. He opened the window of the hotel room, and here's what he said:

"I peeked around the window, and he was right there, less than twelve inches away from my face," DeLong said. "It actually made me jump back a little bit."

"The man was crying, sobbing," DeLong said. That's when DeLong's Crisis Intervention Training kicked in, he said. There was no crime being committed; it was time for compassion.

He began to calmly talk to the man, assuring him from the start that he was not in trouble.

"I told him, 'We just want to help you out, but to do that we need you to come inside.'" The back-and-forth seemed to work. The man inched closer to the open window while DeLong repeatedly assured him that he and Hall were there to help.

---

[8]   Brief *Amicus Curiae* of the American Civil Liberties Union, The American Diabetes Association, The Epilepsy Foundation, Mental Health America, The National Disability Rights Network, and the Arc, *et al.*, In Support of Respondent, No. 13-1412 at 1.

[9]   Stuart Tomlinson, *Officers Who Coaxed Intoxicated, Distraught Man From Narrow Ledge of Old Town Hotel Relied on Crisis Training*, The Oregonian/OregonLive, Dec. 4th, 2014.

Slowly, the man moved closer to the open window until he was close enough to touch. Both officers reached out, each grabbing an arm, and pulled the man into the room through the window.

The rescue couldn't have lasted more than a minute or two, DeLong said. Once inside, it became clear the man was in a mental health crisis and also intoxicated. Paramedics from the Portland Fire Bureau were also in the room and later took the man to a hospital for mental health treatment, police officials said. He was not charged with any crime.

"He was at the point where he wouldn't have lasted very much longer on the ledge," DeLong said. Hall and DeLong later learned that the man had crawled out on the narrow ledge on the building's west side, and then side-stepped his way nearly 100 feet around to the building's south side. "It's scary to think about what could have happened," DeLong said.

Just a year ago, that call might have ended very differently. Just a year ago, many calls in Portland just like that ended up with the person on the ledge injured and in jail, or dead. But our settlement has helped prevent needless tragedies because it requires the Crisis Intervention Training that Officer DeLong relied on to help successfully resolve this situation.

In prisons, we've long challenged unconstitutional conditions of confinement. We've also recognized the importance of ADA compliance in prisons and jails, particularly regarding the treatment of prisoners with mental health conditions or other disabilities. In Pennsylvania, we've issued a letter of findings identifying the state's use of solitary confinement and failure to provide treatment for people with serious mental health conditions as both unconstitutional and violative of the ADA. And we've challenged the overuse of solitary confinement on juveniles with disabilities in California and Ohio.

Community Living and Employment

You may have heard about our *Olmstead* enforcement work. The Justice Department is very committed to the civil rights principle of community inclusion for people with disabilities. The ADA requires state and local governments to provide services to people with disabilities in the most integrated setting appropriate for each person. *Olmstead* has been called the *Brown v. Board of Education* of the disability rights movement. It says separate isn't equal and unnecessary segregation is discrimination.

I'm proud to say the Justice Department and disability advocates and lawyers across the country are transforming the paradigm of services that states provide to people with disabilities from one that assumed that people with disabilities were not capable of living in, benefiting from and contributing to the outside community, and that assumed that it would be cheaper to serve everyone in one place. Because of those assumptions, state systems were set up so that people with disabilities had to go to an institution—and be segregated and interact only with other people with disabilities—or they had to go without.

Those assumptions about how best to serve people with disabilities are wrong. First, the cost assumption is wrong—community-based services cost less than institutional ones. And we can serve just about everybody, no matter how complicated his or her needs, in the community. Second, we know that people with disabilities benefit from community inclusion. Community involvement helps people with disabilities—it avoids learned helplessness, stimulates intellectual growth, develops social skills and increases self-esteem. This shouldn't surprise us. A person learns to live in the community by living in the community. We all need supports—family, friends, guides, maps, Google—but we don't learn the community by staying in our room. Integration of people with disabilities also helps the community. Community members learn to accept differences, improve communication skills, and learn from the diversity of experiences of people with disabilities.

Through our *Olmstead* enforcement, we're transforming state service systems from ones that force people into institutions to ones that focus on services provided in a person's home—whether it's their family's home or their own home or a small group of roommates.

Since 2009, we've reached transformative settlement agreements with the states of Georgia, Delaware, Virginia, New York, New Hampshire and North Carolina. Under these agreements, the states must develop community-based services for people with mental health and developmental disabilities and transition people from institutions into the community.[10] These agreements are helping approximately 46,000 people with disabilities reenter or stay in their communities.[11]

At first, our *Olmstead* work focused on where people live. But community integration doesn't end at the door to your apartment. The fact that a person sleeps in the community at night will not mean much if they spend their days in an institution.

We are now applying the community-integration lens to other areas of life, including school, work, and day programs. Last year, we reached an agreement with the state of Rhode Island to transform its employment and day services for people with intellectual and developmental disabilities from one that sent people to sheltered workshops to one that supports people with disabilities in real jobs for real wages.

You can read about Stephen, Pedro, and Louis, some of the people who have benefited from our Rhode Island settlement, on our Faces of *Olmstead* page on www.ada.gov/olmstead. Louis just completed his probation period at work. He earns far more than minimum wage, receives full benefits, and is a union member.

You can read about Peter Maxmean on the front page of the Sunday *New York Times* from December 7, 2014.[12] That article tells how, since leaving the sheltered workshop, Peter found a good-paying job, learned to drive, got his license, bought a car (and got his first parking ticket on the day of our press conference), got engaged, and got married.

Coordination of Federal Programs

We at the Civil Rights Division understand that our enforcement work, alone, can't change the world. For that reason, we're working with

---

[10] The White House, Office of Public Engagement, *Olmstead Champion Meets the President*, at 6. (June 22, 2011), available at http://www.whitehouse.gov/blog/2011/06/22/olmstead-champion-meets-president. (*citing* 28 C.F.R. § 35.130(d)).

[11] Accomplishments Under the Leadership of Attorney General Eric Holder, available at (http://www.justice.gov/accomplishments) (March 2015).

[12] James Estrin, *Love, at Long Last*, Sunday New York Times, Dec. 7th, 2014. (http://lens.blogs.nytimes.com/2014/12/07/love-at-long-last/).

other agencies to address disability discrimination through guidance and coordination of federal programs.

In November 2014, together with the Department of Education, we released a Dear Colleague Letter to public schools across the country explaining that the effective communication requirements of the ADA are not subsumed within the special education requirements of the IDEA. That guidance made clear that in some instances, a school may need to provide auxiliary aids and services to ensure equally effective communication to a student with a disability that are not required under the IDEA.

In our employment-related work we are also working closely with other agencies. The Civil Rights Division is co-leading the Curb Cuts to the Middle Class Initiative, which is a group of eleven agencies working together to coordinate and leverage resources across the federal government to increase middle class employment for people with significant disabilities.

Already, the Curb Cuts Initiative has helped organize a White House Champions of Change event and a White House Summit on employment of people with disabilities. Over the next few months, the initiative will be:

- developing online tools to help bring federal resources to job seekers with disabilities and the companies that want to hire them;
- implementing job-driven strategies to help people with disabilities develop the skills they need for today's and tomorrow's high-demand careers; and
- increasing collaborations among American Job Centers, educational institutions, labor unions, vocational rehabilitation (VR) agencies, veterans' organizations, independent living centers, and others to offer career path employment supports.

Conclusion

We have some unprecedented opportunities before us right now to level the playing field for people with disabilities in all areas of life, but it will take all of us working together. Working with all of you, as well as with other federal agencies, service providers, and the private sector, the Civil Rights Division stands ready to do its part to break down the barriers faced by people with disabilities.

Mother Teresa said, "I alone cannot change the world, but I can cast a stone across the waters to create many ripples." I rarely encourage people to cast stones, but I look forward to creating ripples–even waves– of equal opportunity with all of you.

The Litigation Landscape

Laurence Paradis[1]

Disability rights advocacy in the legislative and litigation arena is an exciting area because our movement is the current successor to the civil rights movement of the 1960s, and we are at that moment where African-Americans were forty years ago. What we do today will have transformative impact. I will discuss a few examples of areas where progress has been made but so much more is needed.

Transportation

I start with transportation. Buses have been transformed for physical access. People put their bodies on the line and lay down in the streets and protested and went to jail. We had our Selma movements, and we're still having them, and they have had real world impact.

However, there is so much of the transportation system that remains virtually inaccessible. One example is sidewalk access. The curb cut is the universal symbol for access. We have achieved a world where, in most cities, there are a good number of curb cuts. However, in almost every city, county, and state, there are tens of thousands of inaccessible sidewalks in every part of their system. I was in New York City recently. In southern Manhattan, I could not go two blocks in a wheelchair without risking my life and limb, because at every corner the curb cuts that existed were crumbling and were impossible to use without somebody steadying my chair and pushing me. That should not be, and that cannot be permitted to continue.

---

[1] Laurence Paradis is the executive director of Disability Rights Advocates.

To fix this is going to require concerted effort. We have been waiting far too long for federal agencies to finalize regulations and access standards for sidewalks. At this point, it feels like *Waiting for Godot*. We have had great successes in several cases forcing cities and state agencies to remedy sidewalk access barriers, but we have had to do so by convincing the courts to act in the absence of express federal standards. Moreover, in San Francisco, a Court recently ruled against the plaintiff in a sidewalk access case in part because the judge noted there are still no finalized standards from federal regulators on sidewalk access. We need to pressure federal agencies to finalize and issue such standards as binding federal law.

In terms of the light rail and heavy rail systems, we are still stuck in a model called the key station concept that the ADA accepted twenty-five years ago that said a little bit of access was good enough. Well, it's not good enough. Having only key stations accessible does not really make the system accessible. In twenty-five more years, we need to see universal access to all major transportation systems, and that requires some legislative change.

The air travel system is essentially inaccessible if you are in a wheelchair. The level of access is abysmal, with literally no access onboard almost every airplane flying through the country. For many wheelchair users, just flying across the country remains extremely difficult. There are many wheelchair users who cannot do it at all. The Air Carrier Access Act is not really an access act; it's a dis-access act that says we should not expect access. That has to change.

What's icing on the cake is that what little standards the Air Carrier Access Act has are not enforceable through litigation by individuals whose rights are violated. The courts have held that the Air Carrier Access Act has no private right of action. This brings to mind an old joke from Annie Hall. Two elderly women are at a Catskill mountain resort, and one of them says, "Boy, the food here is terrible." The other one says, "Yeah, I know, and such small portions." That's how I feel about Air Carrier Access Act.

Taxis are just another example of inaccessible transportation. Where did we agree that an entire form of mass transit could be completely inaccessible forever? That was a compromise accepted in the enactment of the ADA that taxis don't have to be accessible even if they are new unless they are in what is called a van. Most taxis are not in vans; therefore, throughout the country almost every taxi continues to be inaccessible. We did have one bright moment of victory in New York City last year where we were able to argue that the new taxis in the city were vans, and as a result, we were able to get half of the 10,000 taxis in that fleet to be made accessible within seven years. But that is just one city. In every other city in the country, the taxi system is abysmal for physical access.

For blind people, taxi service is generally more usable because they do not need wheelchair accessible features. What they do need, however, are policies that ensure that drivers do not reject a passenger because of the presence of a service dog. We've made a little bit of progress by enforcing this law for regular taxis, but it's being undercut by disruptive new technologies such as Uber that come in and replace the taxi systems. Not only do these new transportation providers provide virtually no wheelchair accessible vehicles, but they also don't enforce the laws that require drivers to stop and pick up blind people with guide dogs. That cannot be tolerated. We are fighting that issue right now in a case against Uber.

Technological Innovation

New technologies need to have access as a minimum requirement before they are allowed to transform our economy. The regulators are far too slow in finishing their job of establishing regulations for access to new technologies such as the Internet. Once again, we have had to ask the courts to enforce the ADA in areas where the regulations are decades behind. As a result, several courts have held that the ADA does not apply to purely Internet-based commercial enterprises.

There has been a lot of talk about the *Scribd* case.[2] It's an important precedent in that it properly held that the existing ADA does apply to the world of e-commerce. The court in that case got the point of the ADA. The court held:

> The ADA was the most sweeping civil rights legislation
> since the Civil Rights Act of 1964. When it was enacted,

---

[2] *Nat'l Fedn. of the Blind v. Scribd Inc.*, 2015 U.S. Dist. LEXIS 34213 (D. Vt. 2015).

Congress had no conception of how the Internet would change global commerce. * * * Now that the Internet plays such a critical role in the personal and professional lives of Americans, excluding disabled persons from access to covered entities, that use it as their principal means of reaching the public, would defeat the purpose of this important civil rights legislation.[3]

The *Scribd* case will hopefully help transform access to the Internet. *Forbes* magazine, in commenting on this decision, wrote,

The court's conclusion seems to apply equally to all other online content retailers, a universe of tens of thousands of sites and could extend to every online retailer. That makes the opinions' reach breathtaking with enormous implications. . . . [Many] websites do not comply with the ADA today and the ADA is murky about what compliance requires. As a result, many thousands of websites may have to incur substantial remediation expenses to comply with the ADA. In the interim, this opinion could produce a litigation tsunami against sites that aren't in compliance.[4]

We want that tsunami if that is what it takes to achieve equal access to this critical area of life!

There is a problem when access is not built into the new technologies that are coming to change our world today and will continue to change our world every year up through ADA 50. If we don't get access built in at the beginning, we will always be fighting against this argument that it's too costly. That's the battle we need to overcome. Sharing ideas and strategies is critical in that fight to overcome inaccessibility.

---

[3] *Id.* at 24-27.

[4] Eric Goldman, *Scribd Must Comply With The Americans With Disabilities Act*, Forbes Magazine (March 26th, 2015), available at http://www.forbes.com/ sites/ericgoldman/2015/03/26/scribd-must-comply-with-the-americans-with-disabilities-act/

Education

There are so many other fights where we are struggling every day in the trenches to enforce basic rights to access. For example, in education there is a fight for access to textbooks. It's mind boggling that every year we're still fighting for whether students with sensory disabilities should have the same right to have their course materials at the same time in accessible formats as other students. The University of Pennsylvania settlement with the DOJ was a good start. That's one university out of thousands, and the rest are not doing so well.

Prejudice in the world of higher education against students who are blind, deaf, or have other disabilities is continuing to run rampant. We had a case against Boston University where the head of that university said, well, if you have a learning disability, there's a community college down the road that should be just fine for you. The judge in that case issued a finding that that was blatant discrimination. That was ten to fifteen years ago.

Today we have a school arguing that a blind person who has dedicated his life to becoming a medical clinician could not be a safe chiropractor. That case was *Cannon v. Palmer College.*[5] Scott LaBarre obtained a wonderful victory in that case, establishing that a blind student can be a safe chiropractor. This case reveals how far we still have to go to achieve equal access in higher education and in the professions.

Employment

Just two months ago in New York City, we settled a case against the city police department. It had adopted a policy that no police officer could be employed if they used a hearing aid to mitigate their hearing loss. The city agreed to drop that policy, but only after we sued them and were literally at the courthouse steps waiting for the trial to begin. I could only conclude the city had a come to Jesus moment. This case, like many, shows how far we have to go to achieve real progress in overcoming the historical disparities in employment for people with disabilities.

---

[5] *Palmer College of Chiropractic v. Davenport Civ. Rights Comm'n*, 850 N.W.2d 326 (Iowa 2014).

Housing

In terms of housing, so much needs to be done. Again, where did we decide that almost all single family housing in this country could be completely inaccessible to anyone in a wheelchair? That is the norm today. There is a movement slowly beginning known as the fight for "visitability," which says that new housing should at least allow a wheelchair user to get in the door and use the bathroom. This is just the beginning of a necessary fight to open the door to access in a fundamental part of life—the homes we live in. It's a fight we have to fight.

Criminal Justice

The criminal justice system continues to basically warehouse many people with mental and developmental disabilities. Police continue to disregard the needs of people with clear mental disorders, leading to unnecessary and excessive force. The Sheehans in the world are going to continue to suffer and die unless we do something about that.[6]

The use of solitary confinement against youth with disabilities continues to be rampant, and the school to prison pipeline has to be stopped. Many of us are working to change this system, and it's critical we achieve such changes.

Universal design remains an important goal. We talk about it. We need to make it the law.

Changing the Paradigm

The common mainstream culture continues to look at us in views of either pity or heroics. We shouldn't have to be heroes in order to get on a bus, get on a train, go to work, or be treated the same as everyone else. This is an exciting time for our movement because so much progress is being achieved in so many different parts of life. There is an emerging disability rights culture that is challenging the mainstream myths and

---

[6] *City & Cnty. of San Francisco v. Sheehan*, 135 S. Ct. 1765 (2015).

stereotypes. The word "disability pride" is becoming a notion where we're starting to say, I'm disabled and I'm proud. I'm not a hero, but I'm dealing with it, and I just want to be treated the same as others and have equal opportunities to participate and succeed. To mention a few examples, there has been some progress on access to sports, but we need to expand on this and also have access to art, music, fashion, and all cultural aspects of society.

There are many other crucial fights for rights we need to pursue. For example, we are going to win the battle over pregnancy discrimination in the next five years. We have good allies there. Pregnancy is a temporary disability, and it shouldn't mean that you have to weigh your job versus being able to take a few months off to take care of your child.

Similarly, we need to ensure real enforcement of rights against genetic discrimination.

It is also key that we address the issue of affordability of new technologies. Technology has opened up so many opportunities in so many ways in terms of adaptive technologies, adaptive software programs, high tech wheelchairs, and so forth. But what good is such technology if you can't afford it? Right now there's a campaign called Users First, fighting to make sure people can get insurers to cover a wheelchair that will actually work and get them mobile in the community. I know so many disabled people trapped in their homes because insurers will not cover adequate reliable wheelchairs. If we are trapped in our homes, it's just another form of civil confinement.

We often look to veterans because society supports veteran rights, disabled veterans in particular. We need to enforce the right of veterans with PTSD to get suicide prevention care. Too often, such veterans are literally dying due to an inadequate system of veterans' health care. We went to trial on that issue, achieved a major victory, and the federal Ninth Circuit Court of Appeals then threw out our victory and said veterans have no right to go to court to enforce their due process rights under the Constitution. That is an affront to us all.

Jurisprudence

My final point pertains to jurisprudence. Currently, the Supreme Court has held that the states are free to discriminate against people with disabilities without being held to pay monetary damages. That is because we have been trapped in the constitutional standard of what's called "rational basis minimum scrutiny." This has been the standard we have had to live under ever since the Supreme Court in the *Cleburne* case in 1985 said that the disabled people in that case, the mentally retarded (the term used then) should only be entitled to what's called rational basis scrutiny.[7] The holding in *Cleburne* has been followed in many subsequent court decisions, including the Supreme Court decision in *Board of Trustees of the University of Alabama v. Garrett* in 2001 where a woman who took time off to be treated for breast cancer was denied her job when she returned to work.[8] In a 5-4 decision, Judge Rehnquist held that the state could not be liable for discrimination against such people with disabilities. Judge Rehnquist stated in his decision that "State entities could quite hard headedly and perhaps hard heartedly hold to job requirements which do not make allowance for the disabled."[9] That's the kind of attitudes and outright discrimination that we are still fighting day-to-day.

Finally, we need to enforce the rights that are on paper. What good is a right without enforcement? Five judges on our Supreme Court currently do not believe that we should be able to enforce many of our civil rights laws, and they have undercut enforcement mechanisms through procedural decisions affecting the ability to achieve real progress. This calls for effective electoral action to achieve positive changes to the court over time.

I hope that when the ADA reaches the age of fifty we won't be fighting so many of the same fights for equal access. I hope by then our society will be a true model for the rest of the world of what full equality and opportunity can mean. We need to sign on to the international convention. We need to achieve a society where disability is just one aspect of the continuum of our world and where no one is denied equal access or opportunity because of such disability.

---

[7] *City of Cleburne, Texas v. Cleburne Living Center, Inc.,* 473 U.S. 432 (1985).

[8] *Bd. of Trs. of the Univ. of Ala. v. Garrett,* 531 U.S. 356 (2001).

[9] *Id.* at 367-68.

Convention on the Rights of Persons with Disabilities

Christopher Slobogin[1]

One hundred and fifty countries have ratified the Convention on the Rights of People with Disabilities.[2] President Barack Obama signed it in 2009, and even though it did not initially pass in the Senate, it lost by only five votes, and there are currently attempts to reintroduce it.[3] It is important to consider the Convention, first, because the world is behind it and, hopefully, the United States will join it, and, second, because its provisions are very similar to the provisions of the Americans with Disabilities Act.

In particular, I want to focus on the Convention's impact on laws that have to do with mental disability, and specifically laws having to do with mental disability and deprivations of liberty and property. The provisions of the Convention on this issue are radical, at least compared to what we usually think of as mental health law, because the Convention would eliminate all laws that are based on mental disability or have

---

[1] Christopher Slobogin occupies the Milton R. Underwood Chair in Law at the Vanderbilt Law School. He also holds a secondary appointment as an affiliate professor of psychiatry in the Vanderbilt School of Medicine.

[2] Daniel Dickinson, *Treaty on Rights of Persons with Disability is ratified by 150 countries*, News & Media: United Nations Radio (2014), available at http://www.unmultimedia.org/radio/english/2014/09/treaty-on-rights-of-persons-with-disability-is-ratified-by-150-countries/#.VaP5AmDtR4c.

[3] Louis Jacobson, *Obama signs, submits treaty, but Senate hasn't ratified it yet*, Tampa Bay Times (2008). Updated by Louis Jacobson, *38 Republicans vote against ratification, but treaty could get another vote next year*, Tampa Bay Times (2012). Available at http://www.politifact.com/truth-o-meter/promises/obameter/promise/88/sign-the-un-convention-on-the-rights-of-persons-wi/.

mental disability as a predicate. There are literally hundreds of these kinds of laws in the United States. We have involuntary hospitalization. We have the insanity defense. We have guardianship laws. And there are many others. The Convention would require all these laws to be abolished and instead be reframed in terms of disability-neutral criteria. That's a very significant agenda. I believe that it is also consistent with the way the ADA might be construed.

What the Convention does not do is give us a good idea of how its principles would be implemented. What I want to do here is to provide suggested statutory language, which might be a model for implementation of the nondiscrimination policy of the Convention.

The first key provision of the Convention is Article 12, which says: "States shall recognize that persons with disabilities enjoy legal capacity on an equal basis with others in all aspects of life."[4] That's a basic nondiscrimination statement.

What does this mean for people with mental disability? The official commentary to the Convention states that one thing this means is that all special defenses based on mental disability must be abolished. That would include elimination of the insanity defense, which is a special defense to criminal charges for people with mental disability.

In addition, the Convention's language would require elimination of guardianship laws based on mental disability, as well as laws allowing hospitalization of people who have been found incompetent as a result of mental disability. The official commentary says these latter laws should be replaced by "supported decision-making." That process entails ensuring that the individual is the ultimate decision maker on any issue that's to be decided. The individual can be aided by professionals or other individuals, preferably chosen by the person, but the ultimate decision maker is the individual, not a third party. Article 12 requires that supported decision-making take the place of guardianship and other incompetency laws.[5]

---

4   Article 12 – Equal recognition before the law: Available at http://www.un.org/disabilities/default.asp/default.asp?id=272

5   http://www.un.org/disabilities/convention/conventionfull.shtml

Another key provision of the Convention is Article 14, which states: "The existence of a disability shall in no case justify a deprivation of liberty."[6] This article asserts, as the commentary says, that detention is "unlawful" when it "is grounded in the combination between mental or intellectual disability and other elements such as dangerousness or care and treatment."[7] In effect, what this article requires is the abolition of both police power commitment and commitment based on mental disability and danger to self.

Article 14 would essentially eliminate all mental health laws as we've come to know them. How can this be implemented? Most of the points below are from a book I published with Harvard University Press in 2006 entitled *Minding Justice: Laws that Deprive People with Mental Disability of Life and Liberty* (Harvard University Press 2006).[8] My proposals in that book are consistent with the Convention, because I argue that laws should no longer reference diagnosis or mental disability, but instead should focus on the precise dysfunctions or functions that the law considers legally relevant.

In *Minding Justice*, I divided the various contexts mentioned above into three different categories: The punishment context, which encompasses the criminal justice system and issues like the insanity defense; the prevention model, which has to do with laws that involve preventive intervention such as police power civil commitment and so forth; and finally laws meant to protect individuals, such as guardianship laws, incompetency laws, and so on. In each area, I proposed specific statutory language that implements nondiscrimination principles consistent with what the Convention and ADA propose.

Starting with the punishment model, I suggested, consistent with the Convention, that the insanity defense and all other special defenses based on mental disability be abolished and that people with disabilities get the same defenses, no more and no less, as those available to people without mental disability, assuming a criminal justice system based on

---

[6]   Article 14 – Liberty and security of person: Available at http://www.un.org/disabilities/default.asp/default.asp?id=274.

[7]   *Id.*

[8]   Christopher Slobogin, *Minding Justice: Laws that Deprive People with Mental Disability of Life and Liberty* (Harvard University Press 2006).

subjective criminal law. For example, let's say a person is charged with murder. There would be a defense both for persons who did not intend to kill and for those who intended to kill but thought they were being threatened with deadly force by the victim, as with self-defense, or by a third party, as with the duress defense. But there would no longer be a special defense for people with mental disability like the insanity defense.

For some flavor of how this would apply, consider the John Hinckley case. He would not have had a defense under this statute because even under the defense theory of that case, he intended to kill President Reagan, and his motivation was to impress Jodie Foster.[9] Under no stretch of the imagination is it justifiable to kill a person in order to impress an actress; therefore, he would not have a defense. On the other hand, Daniel M'Naghten, whose name graces the most famous test for insanity, tried to kill the prime minister of England thinking the prime minister of England was trying to kill him, so he would have a defense.[10]

This is a very controversial proposal, and there is much more to say on the topic. The point I want to make here is that this formulation is consistent with the Convention, because it does not differentiate between people with mental disability and people who do not have mental disability. I call it the "integrationist test" because it integrates defenses for people with mental disability with defenses that are generally available to everyone.

The prevention model involves situations where the state is intervening preventively to keep harm from occurring to another individual. There are basically three criteria here. The first is that no one can be subjected to preventive intervention unless the criminal justice system does not have jurisdiction, as when a person has been acquitted by reason of insanity, has an infectious disease, is an enemy combatant, or has been released from prison and has not committed a new criminal offense. In all other cases, dangerous people would have

---

[9]   *United States v. Hinckley*, 672 F.2d 115 (D.C. Cir. 1982); *see also*, Doug Linder, *The Trial of John W. Hinckley, Jr.* (2008) Available at http://law2.umkc.edu/faculty/projects/ftrials/hinckley/hinckleyaccount.html.

[10]   https://www.law.cornell.edu/wex/insanity_defense.

to be dealt with by the criminal justice system or not at all. Second, the person has to be considered dangerous.

The important requirement for our purposes is the third one–the risk has to be the result of what I call undeterrability. I define that term very narrowly. Obviously, one could argue that anyone who has ever committed a crime is undeterrable, but that's not my definition. My definition consists of three types of undeterrability. The first encompasses people who literally do not think they're committing a crime at the time they commit it. This category could include someone with psychosis who is killing innocent people but thinks he's killing space aliens out to get him, or enemy combatants who are under orders to kill and under international law are not committing a crime. The second category of undeterrable individuals are people who cannot prevent the kind of harm they're causing because they have no control over their body, like a person with epileptic seizures, or a person with a contagious disease. The third kind of undeterrability encompasses persons who are willing to cause harm even if serious punishment or serious bodily injury is a highly likely result. This category includes the highly impulsive sex offender or terrorists willing to kill for ideological reasons. This is the kind of person who would cause harm even if a police officer were standing at their elbow.

The prevention model of liberty deprivation is also highly controversial, and there is a lot to discuss regarding this topic. For present purposes, as one can see from the examples above, all three undeterrability categories are applicable to both people with mental disability and to people who do not have mental disability and thus are consistent with the Convention.

We come now to the protection model. Here I'm not sure that my proposals are as consistent with the Convention as the other two models are. The Convention seems to say that even people with severe impairments should be allowed to make their own decisions. I can't agree with that. For instance, a person who randomly nods yes or no when responding to questions should not be allowed to make decisions about important matters, because their "decision" is not reflective of their true desires and makes a mockery of the concept of autonomy.

As with many other thinkers, I would instead require that the person have a minimal understanding of the risks and benefits of the decision, and that we inquire into the reasons for the person's decisions. Unlike many thinkers, I would only require that the person give a reason for their decision, that the person's reasons not be demonstrably false and that the person consider the pros and cons of the decision. Some definitions of competency focus on whether the decision is reasonable or on whether the decision is consistent with the decision of lawyers or doctors. I do not take that approach. Instead I merely require a minimal understanding of the risks and benefits of the decision, that the reasons for acting not be delusional, and that the person not be so clinically depressed that they're not willing to consider the risks and benefits.

All of these points are developed in detail in *Minding Justice* and my recent article, *Eliminating Mental Disability as a Legal Criterion in Deprivation of Liberty Cases: The Impact of the Convention on the Rights of Persons with Disabilities on the Insanity Defense, Civil Commitment, and Competency Law.*[11]

---

[11] Christopher Slobogin, *Eliminating Mental Disability as a Legal Criterion in Deprivation of Liberty Cases: The Impact of the Convention on the Rights of Persons with Disabilities on the Insanity Defense, Civil Commitment, and Competency Law* (July 1, 2014). Vanderbilt Public Law Research Paper No. 14-23. Available at SSRN:http://ssrn.com/abstract=2461279 or http://dx.doi.org/10.2139/ssrn.2461279. Also at. Int J Law Psychiatry. 2015 May-Jun;40:36-42. doi: 10.1016/j.ijlp.2015.04.011. Epub 2015 May 8.

Education: School-to-Prison Pipeline

Arlene Mayerson[1]

When I started in the field thirty-six years ago, there were a handful of lawyers in the country that would identify themselves as disability rights lawyers. Many lawyers did disability benefits, but there were few who even knew that there was such a thing as disability civil rights. The reason is simple. There were no disability civil rights until the Section 504 and IDEA regulations were published in 1977.

I have spent most of my waking hours thinking and talking about disability rights in the last thirty-five years. I have so many ideas that I would love to discuss—the ADA, models of equality, how to expand civil rights to human rights, which includes income equality, identity politics, Congressional politics, etc.

I have chosen to focus my remarks on the education of disabled children, an area in crisis. DREDF is currently deeply involved in the School-to-Prison Pipeline (STPP) work, particularly focused on black students with disabilities. We convened a meeting for the National Council on Disability on this topic, drafted a report to be submitted to Congress, and advocate for hundreds of parents and students faced with suspensions and expulsions. Disabled students are twice as likely to be suspended from school as nondisabled students, and black students with

---

[1] Arlene Mayerson has been the directing attorney of the Disability Rights Education & Defense Fund (DREDF) since 1981.

disabilities are four times as likely.[2] Up to 85 percent of incarcerated youth have disabilities, often undiagnosed and unserved in school.[3]

The School-to-Prison Pipeline crisis has generated a lot of attention from the media, government, foundations, politicians, civil rights organizations, lawyers, etc. The President's initiative, My Brother's Keeper (MBK), issued a task force report, which recommends various interventions primarily targeted at black boys. Disabled students are not addressed. Yet, all of the educational strategies and interventions come from the special education playbook. Everyone is abuzz with talk of Positive Behavioral Interventions and Supports, as though it is a new thing, even though it was developed and tested in special education for at least two decades. When criticism was made that girls were not included in MBK, Jim Shelton, head of the task force, stated:

> In special education they have this thing called 'universal design for learning.' It basically says that once you figure out how to design something well for a special-needs population you can actually take those design principles and do it in a way that actually benefits everyone," he said. "I very much believe this process is like that. What are the specific needs of this population, boys and young men of color, but in doing so [identifying those needs] we are creating an infrastructure that actually will benefit everyone." He went on to say, "That will allow you to identify vulnerable populations who are disproportionately boys and young men of color, but are not exclusively boys and young men of color. That will benefit girls of color. That will benefit young white boys

2 U.S. Department of Education Office for Civil Rights, "Civil Rights Data Collection, Data Snapshot: School Discipline" Issue Brief, March 2014. Available at:_http://www2.ed.gov/about/offices/list/ocr/docs/crdc-discipline-snapshot.pdf (last accessed July 7 2015).

3 National Council on Disability. "National Disability Policy: A Progress Report." 2011, http://www.ncd.gov/progress_reports/Oct312011#_edn92.

who have issues that are causing them to be chronically absent or to be on a path to dropping out of school.[4]

How do you like that! If you read the MBK task force report, you will see that best practices are those developed and piloted by special education. Yet this history is not mentioned. Let's face it; the drafters of the report did not think referencing the special education origins of the suggested remediation would strengthen the document.

Moreover, there is a common misperception that MBK initiatives were designed for black boys, not disabled black boys.

For example, recently, in working to address the STPP, the district sent us a notice of plans for increasing equity through a special summer academy for African-American boys transitioning from middle school to high school. When the parent of one of our clients with a mental health disability impacting behaviors expressed interest, she was told that this was not a program for students that needed special education support.

This response perfectly illustrates the problems with the "us and them" silo mentality that pervades education. All of the students in the academy should have the benefit of individualized supports and differentiated education. The nondisabled students were being treated like a monolith, with a one size fits all approach to what was supposed to be a remedial program.

For years, those of us who litigate and influence legislation on special education have stressed that disabled kids should have access to the general classroom. Now, I think the tables should be turned. General educators need to learn the lessons of special education: differentiated education, adaptations to curriculum, and positive functional behavioral assessments and implementation plans. We need one unified system of universally designed education for all students utilizing the concepts well known to educators of students with disabilities and people with disabilities. Disability education principles should be in the forefront.

---

4   Jonathan Capehart, "The Promise of My Brother's Keeper," *Washington Post*, July 22, 2014. Available at: http://www.chicagomanualofstyle.org/tools_citationguide.html (last accessed July 7, 2015).

Which leads me to a big issue and question.

If you read the civil rights academic literature, you will see a strong almost uniform agreement that the worst thing that could happen to a black student is to be labeled disabled and put in special education. I say "put in" because special education is seen as a place, like a dungeon with no escape. The stigma of disability is seen as too negative for the questionable outcomes. IDEA is even seen as a sinister vehicle to re-segregate after *Brown*.[5] IDEA is seen as part of the problem not part of the solution. Now, don't get me wrong, over-classification, misclassification, low expectations, excessive suspensions, and terrible outcomes make this an easy conclusion to draw.[6] But lurking alongside this truth is another one, not expressed: Disability is feared and loathed; disabled children are bullied and often left out. This raises a thorny question: Whether to advocate for identification and IDEA eligibility for minority, particularly black students?

We are confronted with the reality of these thorny issues every day at DREDF. Our extraordinary parent advocate unit has many Black and Hispanic clients whose kids are failing, being suspended, becoming disaffected from school, and they fear these students are headed down

---

[5] Erevelles, Nirmala. *Disability and difference in global contexts: Enabling a transformative body politic.* Palgrave Macmillan, 2011. ("Why do supporters of *Brown* not recognize how the assigned status of disability could serve as a mechanism for re-segregating students of color in otherwise desegregated schools?").

[6] For example, in 2010–2011, the national graduation rate for students with disabilities was 61 percent, compared to 80 percent for all students. Stetser, Marie C., and Robert Stillwell. "Public High School Four-Year On-Time Graduation Rates and Event Dropout Rates: School Years 2010–11 and 2011–12." April 2014. Available at: http://nces.ed.gov/pubs2014/2014391.pdf (last accessed July 7, 2015). Classification also predicts higher suspension rates for Black students but not for their White peers. Losen, Daniel J., Cheri Hodson, Jongyeon Ee, and Tia E. Martinez (2014). "Disturbing Inequities: Exploring the Relationship Between Racial Disparities in Special Education Identification and Discipline." Available at: http://digitalcommons.library.tmc.edu/childrenatrisk/vol5/iss2/15 (last accessed July 7, 2015). *See also* National Council on Disability. "Breaking the School-to-Prison Pipeline for Students with Disabilities" at 11. Jun. 18, 2015, http://www.ncd.gov/publications/2015/06182015/ (last accessed July 7, 2015) (general discussion of current state of special education).

the STPP. Many of these kids have severe ADHD, LD, and PTSD (often considered "soft" disabilities by detractors) that have not been identified. Often eligibility has been denied, even with an ADHD diagnosis because the school psychologist decides that the student has oppositional defiance disorder. We fight for eligibility for these kids (under the IDEA or 504), because it is their best bet. We fight to get supports in the regular classroom, behavioral and academic support, counseling, and services encompassed within the IDEA. There is simply no other nondisability legal basis to demand these services.

Progressive educators think IDEA has failed and that a unified system of universal design should replace it. This idea includes doing away with the disability label. I am all for a unified system using universal design, but the idea that we should take away the disabled identification worries me. For the first time in the history of the world, a rich positive thriving disability culture is being developed. In fact, I would say it is exploding.

So, I leave you with this question: Do we deprive these students of an identity, a rich history and culture by taking away the disability "label"? How can we create a movement to ensure that schools inculcate disability pride, history, and culture? Can we, as a movement, change the "disability" experience and image so that parents and students, teachers and classmates, and the community do not equate disability and special education with the stigma of inferiority?

The Medical Decision Process

Elizabeth Pendo[1]

The requirement of full and confirmed consent to all medical decisions developed out of a larger movement centering around the rise of autonomy and patients' rights that developed in the 1960s alongside the civil rights movement. Later, the right to free and informed consent was the right to say no or to choose treatment. That principle is probably best embodied in a California Court of Appeals case out of 1986.[2] It's really an example of the prevailing rule that we have today, that competent adults have the right to refuse treatment. Although that case upheld Elizabeth Bouvia's right to refuse treatment, there was disability bias and misinformation on decisions of capacity and how we view decisions made by people with disabilities. The language of the case itself is often cited as an example of disability bias. It was seen as accepting too readily her perceived decision to end her life because they accepted and promoted a devaluation of her life.

As many people have noticed about this case, the perceived quality of her life, at least as framed by the court, really had more to do with prejudice and a lack of appropriate supports for living with a disability than it had to do with her actual disability itself. Those themes of assumptions, false beliefs, devaluation of life, continue to have a lot of resonance around the so-called right to die when invoked by people with disabilities. It's a complicated issue.

---

[1]   Elizabeth Pendo is vice dean and professor of law at Saint Louis University School of Law. She has a secondary appointment as professor of health management and policy at Saint Louis University School of Public Health, and is a member of the Center for Health Law Studies and the William C. Wefel Center for Employment Law at the School of Law.

[2]   *Bouvia v. Superior Court*, 179 Cal. App. 3d 1127 (2nd App. District 1986).

These cases focusing on autonomy also highlight the legal issue of competency. It's a troubling concept. Generally in healthcare it means the ability to understand the medical problem and its consequences, to evaluate options, to communicate a choice to your healthcare providers.

Incompetency is of course a legal concept. Only a court declares someone incompetent or unable to make his or her own decisions. This is an interesting conversation to have with doctors, which I do frequently, because they often believe that they make that determination, when, in fact, a court does. They can appoint or recognize a substitute decision maker, right?

My research has been focused on looking at the experiences of people with disabilities in the healthcare system that have not been declared unable to make their own decisions, but still experience barriers and limitations in making their own decisions.

Other components of the classic legal landscape include a basic division of case law and legal thinking on capacity into two categories: people who have never had decisional capacity from birth and people who once had decisional capacity and now do not or are perceived to not have decisional capacity. A lot of attention in bioethics and health law and in the courts is given to these two categories. Think of the Nancy Cruzan case in Missouri[3] or the Terri Schiavo case in Florida.[4] The cases that go to court are almost always women, and they're always presented as certain, static, and lacking in ambiguity. The diagnosis and prognosis are presented as completely clear, which is interesting because it doesn't reflect real life.

For folks who had decisional capacity in the past but have lost it in the present, either on a temporary or permanent basis, there are some formal legal statements they can use: Advanced directives, living wills, and durable powers of attorney for healthcare. These are designed to preserve autonomy in the event that it's lost or threatened or diminished, permanently or temporarily, but we know most people don't complete advanced directives. Also, many states have surrogate decision-making statutes that typically appoint from a list of next of kin to make decisions.

---

[3] *Cruzan v. Harmon*, 760 S.W.2d 408 (Mo. 1988).

[4] *Bush v. Schiavo*, 885 So. 2d 321 (Fla. 2004).

There are still ways in which bias and assumptions creep into decision-making regardless of the legal tools available.

The third major feature of the legal landscape pertains to legal devices for decision-making or situations where decisional capacity is not present or is presumed not to be present. Those are the traditional devices like guardianship or substituted decision-making or a proxy decision maker is appointed in theory to make the decision that the patient would have made if he or she were competent. There are many criticisms of the guardianship process. It's a state law process, so it varies a little bit state to state, but in general, guardianship is a plenary or full process, meaning you lose all rights to all decisions, not just healthcare. A person with a disability who goes through the guardianship process loses autonomy in all areas. It's been criticized as anti-therapeutic, as stigmatizing, as being used inappropriately to take away the legal right to make decisions, often on insufficient evidence because it can vary state to state what type of evidence is acceptable, and although it's intended in most states to take into account the patient's subjective wishes, conversations around these preferences are notoriously difficult. That's why the vast majority of people do not complete any form of advanced directive. It's very hard to discuss what you might want in a hypothetical situation that you are not actually in. Again, there's still a way that assumptions and biases can creep up.

Of course there's the newer model of supported decision-making, where a third-party assists people to make their own decision. This is an incredibly interesting idea because it is not particular to people with disabilities. It really is intended to mirror the decision-making process generally, how we all make decisions, even big decisions. We seek advice, we look for input and information from friends or family or professionals who might know more about this, and then we make our own decision. It could be especially promising for people with intellectual or developmental disabilities, although, again, it's a universal model that could work in a lot of different situations, like for use with children, developing minors, or the elderly. In contrast to guardianship, it's seen as empowering; the patient retains their right to make decisions. It also seems more consistent with legal rights and human rights as expressed in the Convention on the Rights of Persons with Disabilities. It is a newer model, and there have been some concerns raised about the risk of undue influence by these third parties. Blumenthal, Kohn, and Campbell have written about the empirical evidence of supported decision-making, the process, the techniques, the outcomes, and the risks, a side note as to nothing is perfect.[5]

The entire landscape is characterized by the risk of disability bias, of incorrect and negative assumptions about life with a disability. Bias really runs throughout this landscape and can enter at various points, notwithstanding certain legal structures and devices designed to minimize it other than supported decision-making.

In my work, I have noticed there is a lot of focus on the most dramatic, perhaps the most extreme, factual situations. They are often presented as much known, very black and white, and very static. My work in the healthcare system just does not reveal that that is very often the situation. There is a lot less focus on everyday interactions and decisions that are less clear and perhaps more complex. In the world of bioethics, when a doctor's perspective is taken into account, it's very often at the beginning or end of life, and there is a lot less attention to living your life every day. Most of my recent work is focused on everyday clinical encounters and influences on medical decision-making for people with disabilities who have decisional capacity. I think attitudes and biases lead to disparities. They also limit choices patients have and choices patients make, and can constrain medical decision-making.

My recent research is focused on people with mobility disabilities and inaccessibility to exam equipment, imaging equipment, scales, chairs, tables, and obviously this could apply in other areas.

My research shows that patients with disabilities, especially with mobility disabilities, experience really fundamental physical barriers in healthcare offices and facilities, including a lack of accessible medical and diagnostic equipment, coupled with a lack of policies and procedures designed to accommodate needs and promote access. This is tied to the underlying attitudinal barriers, in particular clinician assumptions, biases, and lack of knowledge about living with a disability. Also, a lack

---

[5]   Nina A. Kohn, Jeremy A. Blumenthal, & Amy T. Campbell, *Supported Decision-Making: A Viable Alternative to Guardianship?*, Penn. State L. Rev., Vol. 117, No. 4 (2013).

of awareness of the Americans with Disabilities Act and federal laws that protect and promote accessible healthcare that really accompanies and underlies these physical barriers. Lawyers love to suggest that we should have a law about something. What I think is fascinating about this area is, we do have a law about this, and we've had it since 1990. What is going on? Something else is going on. I'm interested in the something else and how it affects medical decision-making.

Clinicians experience the same biases and limited thinking that we do generally, but the Institute of Medicine issued a report: *Disability in America*, and the authors identified lack of disability awareness and provider education as among the most significant barriers to care, ahead of insurance coverage and cost.[6] A body of research on the role of cognitive bias and emotions in interacting with people with disabilities really underscores the significance of those barriers. We know if we listen to the experiences of people with disabilities that they report negative encounters with clinicians, ranging from overt discrimination to subtle expressions of paternalism or exclusion or diminishment. Those could be more obvious, but their impact of clinician attitude can also be more subtle and difficult to pinpoint because it's really more structural and subtle.

Bias and negative assumptions can impact communication within the clinician-patient relationship. Mary Catherine Beech and Debra Roder have done interesting work about attitudes of respect and how it influences communication behaviors. They can diminish the essential trust that scholars have deemed critical to the therapeutic relationship. Consider everyday examples like a clinician speaking to a family member rather than to the patient who has a disability, or a recent article in *Health Affairs*, which described a doctor who spoke very slowly, as if his patient may not understand him merely because the patient had a stutter.[7] The article looked at how that affected the relationship not only with that patient but the relationship with the other doctor who also experienced stuttering unbeknownst to doctor number one.

---

[6] Available at http://iom.nationalacademies.org/Activities/SelectPops/Disability InAmerica

[7] Leana S. Wen, *A Simple Case of Chest Pain: Sensitizing Doctors to Patients with Disabilities*, Health Affairs, Vol. 33, No. 10 (Oct. 2014).

Adrienne Ash described that a lack of knowledge and awareness can also diminish the quality of care.[8] If we're relying on clinicians to provide us with full informed consent, they simply can't advise on futures that they can't imagine.

Disability can also function as a distraction from the patient's needs, which may or may not even be related to the disability. In my research on equipment, I found that a lot of healthcare providers believe, falsely, that women with mobility disabilities are not sexually active and are not or should not be mothers; therefore, they just assume that patients with mobility disabilities do not need services offered to other patients, such as screening for STDs or discussion of birth control or discussion of fertility and having children.

Another example that came up more recently is that women with disabilities are less likely to have had a mammogram.[9] Research identifies several different barriers. One is the lack of explicit recommendation from a healthcare provider. Communication from a healthcare provider is an important motivator in mammogram adherence behavior. A study in the American Journal of Public Health published last year looked at reasons for this disparity by comparing experiences of women with and without disabilities, and they used a state mammography registry to study this.[10] They looked for women who had already been to a screening. There is a suggestion that issues of coverage and physical access were not barriers.

The researchers looked at women who didn't come back and sent them letters asking them why. The study finds, to the surprise of absolutely no one, that women with disabilities report barriers similar to those reported by women without disabilities but at a higher rate. What I thought was incredibly interesting is the study also found that women with disabilities are less likely to receive a physician recommendation for

---

[8] Adrienne Asch, *Distracted by Disability*, Cambridge Quarterly of Healthcare Ethics, 7 (1998).

[9] *Women with Disabilities and Breast Cancer Screening*, available at http://www.cdc. gov/ncbddd/disabilityandhealth/pdf/fs_disabilities_breastcancer.pdf.

[10] Bonnie C. Yankaskas, Pamela Dickens, *et al.*, American Journal of Public Health, *Barriers to Adherence to Screening Mammography Among Women with Disabilities*, American J. of Public Health, Vol. 100, No. 5, pp. 947-953 (May 2010).

a screening mammogram even controlling for age.[11] There is something going on in the information being provided to patients that limits the choices and the information that the patients have, and we know from the research that that impacts the choices that patients make.

The literature clearly suggests that disability matters in clinical relationships and treatment recommendations and outcomes often in ways that raise ethical concerns. The literature on cognitive bias suggests that perceptions of disability may inappropriately influence clinicians' medical judgments about conversations and communications about appropriate diagnostic interventions and about treatment. All of that impacts the relationship in which decisions are framed. I see the risk of disability bias in everyday encounters as well as in the more extreme situations that are more often looked at.

Many solutions have been suggested. Obviously enforcing the ADA in the healthcare setting is one suggestion since it was meant to apply there. Somehow that hasn't been noticed enough. There have been significant inroads, but there needs to be more.

Education and training in the Affordable Care Act. The Affordable Care Act also calls for research and data collection on the experiences of people with disabilities in the healthcare system, which could be valuable information.

Something I have been working on lately is reframing appropriate care for people with disabilities as a matter of medical ethics and patient-centered care. Another area to look at, of course, is the inclusion of more clinicians with disabilities and people working on the healthcare system.

---

[11] *Id.*

Accommodations, Telecommunications, Technology, & the Internet of Things

Howard Rosenblum[1]

Reflecting on the future of disability law, I consider three topics. The first is accommodations, the second is telecommunications pursuant to Title IV of the Americans with Disabilities Act, and the third is technology.

With respect to the first item, accommodations, it is important to look at what is being discussed about the attitudes and training of police officers with respect to people with disabilities, which is being looked at now because of the *Sheehan* case in which police officers entered the home of a mentally ill woman without a warrant and ended up almost fatally shooting her.[2]

However, it has to go beyond what was discussed in *Sheehan*. For the next twenty-five years, it has to be more than just police officers who are required to be accommodating toward people with disabilities and adjust their attitudes when they encounter people with disabilities. Beyond police officers, we need to train lawyers from every part of the legal field, as well as judges, doctors, psychologists, and more. All of these people need to understand how to interact with people with disabilities. Even more than that, we need more people who are disabled working in those fields.

When I was twelve, my Jewish mother dragged me to see one of the few deaf attorneys in the country at the time, as he was making a public

---

[1] Howard Rosenblum is chief executive officer at the National Association of the Deaf.

[2] *Sheehan v. City & County of San Francisco*, 743 F.3d 1211 (9th Cir. 2014).

presentation. My mother had been telling me that you can be anything you want to, but best to be a doctor or a lawyer.

I watched as the deaf attorney talked about his experiences in court and the legal world, and a light bulb turned on for me as I realized–wait a minute–I can sue hearing people!

Thanks to that inspiration, I became a lawyer in 1992, which is the birth year of the Americans with Disabilities Act. As I practiced law and litigated in various courts, I encountered many judges unable or unwilling to provide necessary accommodations for me as a deaf attorney or for my clients. These experiences in the courts with intolerant judges made me realize that we need more deaf judges. Generally, we need judges who have disabilities or understand disabilities.

When I met that deaf attorney many years ago, there were only a handful of deaf attorneys at the time. Now we have over 400 deaf attorneys, and I'm sure many more blind attorneys and many more attorneys with disabilities, but it's still not enough. Many of these attorneys with disabilities are encountering barriers when they attempt to get a job. Many of them are not obtaining employment because of discriminatory attitudes. Employers, human resources people, and hiring managers still view us as if we are broken or damaged. We as a group, both disabled and not, have proven that we as legal advocates can damage the institutions that have discriminated against us. We're not damaged, but we sure can do damage.

The second issue, Title IV of the Americans with Disabilities Act, which covers telecommunication access, has been an important one for the deaf community for the past twenty-five years. When I was growing up, we didn't have accessible telephones. I could not call people. At that time, the deaf community had this big green machine that shook the whole house whenever we communicated. However, with that machine I could only call friends of mine who also had the same machine and were deaf. If I wanted to date a hearing girl from my high school, I had to ask my mom to call her. Imagine the embarrassment.

Today we have email, which is great. We have Twitter, Facebook, and other wonderful tools. New technology often adds to our experience. The Video Relay Service, or what is also referred to as Video Interpreting Service, is great. I can call anyone, anytime day or night.

However, with each technology, we face barriers. Every time a new technology is developed, such as the Internet, we struggle with access to it, both the deaf and the blind communities. The Americans with Disabilities Act didn't really apply to the Internet until just recently. We are often retrofitting rather than ensuring access from the start. We are fixing damage that has already been done. The technology should be universally designed from the get-go.

There is a new term in the industry called the Internet of Things, sometimes called "IoT." It means we will not have any privacy anymore. What it really means is that everything will be interconnected. Your smartphone will be connected to your thermostat at home, connected to your lights at your house, connected to the locks on your door (so that you can unlock it for when your kids get home from school), and connected to your car. Your smartphone will be connected to everything you own. I just learned that it will also be connected to your suitcase! We won't lose our suitcases anymore, apparently.

At the same time, the Internet of Things could be beneficial to all people with disabilities, but the benefit depends on whether the engineers take the disabled into consideration and make such technologies accessible to us. If it's purely visual, it doesn't benefit the blind. If it's purely auditory, it doesn't benefit the deaf. There has to be redundancy in every type of technology, which will allow every person with a disability to be able to use the technology.

That's where I think we're going to be in the next twenty-five years when things change. For example, television as we know it will probably not exist twenty-five years from now. People will be watching the Internet, and we might be watching holograms in twenty-five years. Let's imagine a hologram for a moment. How are you going to caption a hologram? We don't know yet. Maybe we will have holographic interpreters.

Through legislation and advocacy, we need to ensure that what we are doing now keeps up with the changing technology. Most federal employees today who are deaf have a hard time making a phone call because they do not have videophones. The technology is already here. Videophones exist. The ADA rule says that videophones are allowable as an auxiliary aid. However, how many federal agencies are actually installing them or implementing effective ones? Many do not due to a failure to understand the need for videophones. Because of this, the National Association of the Deaf sued the IRS, which did not provide effective videophones for deaf employees. We won the lawsuit and obtained a requirement that effective videophones be implemented. Prior to the lawsuit, the IRS provided videophones in 2011, but those videophones were so bad that deaf employees could only call each other internally. The IRS felt that such videophones must be especially fitted with security encryption that renders the devices essentially useless.

During the IRS hearing, I asked their expert witness, "Do you have encryption on the voice phones?" They said no. And I said, "Well, why not?" They said it was considered an allowable security exemption. I said, "Then what's wrong with the videophones? Can't you make that an allowable security exemption as well?" And the expert witness said, "Well, that's above my pay grade."

Looking ahead at the next twenty-five years and beyond, we need comprehensive changes at the federal level to mandate a plethora of successful options to enable people with disabilities to work and access services.

Aging and Disabilities

Julie Nepveu, Susan Silverstein, Dan Kohrman, and Kelly Bagby[1]

Everyone knows that people are living longer than they used to. Everyone used to die when they were thirty and then sixty, and now of course a lot of folks are living past their eighties and in some cases even into their hundreds. There's been a 66 percent increase in people living over 100 years old since 1980.[2] It's just incredible.

In another fifteen years, approximately 20 percent of the population will be over age sixty-five.[3] By the year 2050, thirty-five years from now, we will have 14 million people over the age of eighty-five.[4] That is a huge change, because people over eighty-five start to have a lot more disabilities and a lot more severe disabilities. Approximately half of the people who are going to be over eighty-five will have a severe disability, and for the people who are over sixty-five, about one in four of them will have a disability that is considered severe.

Cognitive and mental health disabilities are, of course, significant among the aged. About 20 percent of people over age fifty-five currently have some sort of mental health concern.[5] In addition to that, we have

---

[1] The authors are senior attorneys for AARP Foundation.

[2] *A Profile of Older Americans: 2012*, U.S. Department of Health and Human Services,

[3] Ortman, Velkoff, & Hogan, *An Aging Nation: The Older Population in the United States: Population Estimates and Projections*, Current Population Reports (May 2014).

[4] *A Profile of Older Americans: 2012*, U.S. Department of Health and Human Services.

[5] *The State of Mental Health and Aging in America*, available at http://www.cdc.gov/aging/pdf/mental_health.pdf

about four-and-a-half million people with Alzheimer's, and by 2050 they're expecting to have 16 million people with Alzheimer's.[6]

About twenty-five percent of the people over age sixty-five will have some sort of mild cognitive impairment without dementia, and they won't know it. We won't know it. We start to lose our functioning when we're about fifty.

Older people don't like to call their circumstances "disabilities," but that is what they are. All the disability rights laws protect them. We encourage people to think about the issues that older people are having as disability issues because the laws don't protect one for aging; they do protect one for disability.

When discussing aging and disability, we consider the Americans with Disabilities Act, but also the Rehabilitation Act and the Fair Housing Act. They all prohibit discrimination that is relevant to an aging population. The basic purposes of these laws include individuality and integration. People have the right to live in the community. People have the right to be treated as individuals, not based on stereotypes, not based on what the characteristics of the group are.

Title II of the Americans with Disabilities Act requires public entities to administer their programs in a way that allows for people to live their most independent lives and to live integrated lives in the community. That means if a state is administering its programs in a way that creates incentives for nursing facility placements, that is illegal. If those people could otherwise live in the community and are eligible for the community and don't oppose moving to the community, then the state has a mandate to move people to the community.

Some of the models that we use to provide services to people as they age and where they will live were developed before the ADA was passed in 1990 and before the pre-ADA Fair Housing Amendments Act, which was added to the Fair Housing Act to include disability. These models are such things as assisted living, continuing care retirement communities, and nursing homes. When counsel for providers raise a "fundamental alteration" defense in negotiations, I have little patience.

---

[6] Alzheimer's Association, *Alzheimer's Disease Facts and Figures*, Alzheimer's & Dementia, Volume 10, Issue 2 (2014).

At a certain point, after thirty years of litigation, I've come to a point of just saying no. Jim Crow didn't work after the early civil rights laws; nobody sat around and said, well, how are we going to work accommodations into Jim Crow.

When Congress passed the ADA, it recognized that one of the most basic rights under the ADA was the right to transportation and equal access to both regular transportation and to paratransit, because if you can't use the regular public transportation, you don't have access to transportation. The reason they recognize it is because it facilitates so many other rights. If you can't get where you're trying to go, you can't go shopping or get a job or visit with your friend or go to healthcare appointments if you don't have transportation.

A lot of folks will have to rely on paratransit. Paratransit is a service available for a three-quarter-mile radius around every fixed route public transportation stop. In some corridors where things are close, it covers everything. It's not a universal service. It won't take you from Annapolis to Baltimore, but it is going to make sure you can get around in the city if you live in the right place. The three-quarter-mile radius is just where they pick up and drop off. That doesn't mean you have to live there. If you can get to three-quarter miles from a transit stop, they have to come and pick you up from there. They have to provide the service.

We are involved with some litigation with the Maryland Disability Law Center. We're suing the state for denying eligibility due to their wait times. People are waiting an hour on the phone to make a ride. If you need a ride, you have to call every day and get a ride, and you have to wait an hour every day. If you need to cancel or change your plans, that's another hour.

There are also issues with sidewalks and curb cuts. Sidewalks have huge holes in them, and the curb ramps, you get down with your wheelchair and then you can't get back up because the angle is too steep or there's a big pothole at the bottom. It is also an issue that people are not clearing the sidewalks of ice and snow.

On March 13, 2015, the United States Department of Transportation issued a new final rule that cleared up a problem that started with a Fifth Circuit Court of Appeals decision, which excused transit providers from providing reasonable accommodations.[7] The Ninth and Second Circuits followed that interpretation.[8] Nine years after this problem started, the DOT's final rule required that transit providers must provide a reasonable accommodation or reasonable modification. The rule applies to both public and private transportation providers too, taxi services, and airport shuttles.

The only place where there is an undue financial and administrative burden defense is for Title II public entities receiving federal funds. Private folks do not have a financial and administrative burden exception.

Everybody knows that integration is a mandate of the ADA. It's also a basic tenet of the Fair Housing Act, the Fair Housing Amendments Act when they added disabilities. We know it prohibits separate accommodations. You can't just push people with disabilities off into the senior housing or off into segregated living facilities. You can't make people live in one section of the neighborhood versus another. You can't only build housing in one section of the community and not another.

The last time AARP polled people on aging, 94 percent of the people it polled said they wanted to age in a place in their community. Nobody wants to leave the place that they're living in now. When landlords look at old people, they often find excuses for eviction or non-renewal of leases. Tenants start to get notices that say things like, you are too old and frail to live here, please look for assisted living. Or you've violated your lease because your house is starting to look messy even though you've been a neat freak your whole life, and therefore we think you should go to a nursing home.

Parallel to the ADA, the Fair Housing Act makes it illegal to deny housing through denial of the sale and rental of housing based on protective classes including "handicap." Also, discrimination in terms of condition is prohibited. Under the Fair Housing Act coverage is broad. One does not have to be the person in the protected class to bring a Fair Housing Act case. For example, if you are the aunt of a person with an

---

[7]   *Melton v. Dallas Area Rapid Transit*, 391 F.3d 669 (5th Cir. 2004).

[8]   *Abrahams v. MTA Long Island Bus*, 644 F.3d 110 (2nd Cir. 2011); *Boose v. Tri-County Metro. Transp. Dist. of Or.*, 587 F.3d 997 (9th Cir. 2009).

intellectual disability who goes to apply for housing and that person is discriminated against, you can file your own fair housing complaint on the basis of the emotional harm and indignity that you had to suffer when you found out that the housing provider misrepresented to your niece that that apartment was not available.

There are provisions in the Fair Housing Act that do not require intent. It is a violation of the Fair Housing Act to advertise, make statements, and provide notices that a reasonable person would interpret as discriminatory. If a fifty-five-plus community or any type of housing or community advertises using pictures that are all of people running and doing Cirque du Soleil poses or pole dancing—and not one picture is of somebody with a white cane or in a wheelchair—that may violate the law.

Protection of individuals from unnecessary nursing home placement is essential. In California we sued on behalf of a class of 38,000 people who were at risk of going into nursing homes because the state had decided to wipe out an entire program that helped people during the day to prevent having to go into institutional care. We were successful.

People are in institutions, and they want to leave. There are 1.5 million people in nursing homes right now.[9] This large number exists despite the establishment of the extensive federal-state Home and Community Based Waiver program. There continue to be incentives to keep profitable beds filled. I have never met a client of mine or of anybody's in a nursing home who can't live in the community. There's not a single person you can show me that with appropriate services wrapped around them couldn't be successful in a community setting. The question is: can we create the momentum to really facilitate that transition for them so that they are successful?

On employment, older workers have challenges not faced by younger workers. Older workers are a growing share of the United States labor force. This is partly because the population of older workers is increasing, and also the proportion of younger workers is barely

---

[9]   John Leland, *Helping Elderly Leave Nursing Homes for a Home*, available at http://www.nytimes.com/2009/09/19/health/policy/19aging.html?_r=0 (Sept. 18, 2009).

increasing; it is even decreasing when you get to workers in the age group below twenty-five.

Over many years, we've seen the growth of workers over fifty on any kind of measure. We've seen the most important trend in the workforce over the last decades is the growth of women participation in the workforce. This increased participation trend is also true of older workers.

There is a very big difference in terms of men and women. The labor force in 1988 was about 12 percent over age fifty-five.[10] It's going to be about double that. It's about a quarter in 2018. Participation at all age levels is gradually increasing, but what's remarkable is that men's participation in the last sixty years, since about 1950, has dropped from about 87 percent participation to only about 70 percent now, whereas women's participation has risen from about a quarter, 27 percent, up to about 60 percent as well.[11]

What makes one think that older workers are worse off? We usually cite the length of time that older workers are out of work. Shockingly, the legislative history of the Age Discrimination and Employment Act of 1967 indicates that trends are remarkably unchanged from the 1960s. Older workers, people over fifty, fifty-five, take about 50 percent longer to find a new job compared to younger workers, and for older workers who are unemployed for particularly long periods of time, that percentage is even higher.[12]

The one embarrassing statistic that we don't like to talk about is that the overall unemployment rate for older workers is lower than the overall unemployment rate for workers generally.[13] The reason for that is

---

[10] *Labor Force Participation Rates of the Population Age 55 and Over, 2011: After the Economic Downturn,* Employee Benefit Research Institute, Vol. 33, No. 2, at 7. (Feb. 2012).

[11] United States Department of Labor, Bureau of Labor Statistics, available at http://www.bls.gov/data/home.htm.

[12] Daniel B. Kohrman, *As More Workers Age, Bias and Insecurities Persist,* Aging Today (Jan. 27, 2014) available at http://www.asaging.org/blog/more-workers-age-bias-and-insecurity-persist.

[13] Emy Sok, *Record Unemployment Among Older Workers Does Not Keep Them Out of the Job Market,* U.S. Bureau of Labor Statistics (March 2010).

largely that in this country we do so poorly by our younger workers, aged eighteen to twenty-five. The unemployment data are just horrifying. That drags the differential between older and younger workers into a place that makes older workers look better off than they are.

Disabilities skew incidence data toward older ages. For example, here is some data about heart disease, hearing loss, and diabetes. About 37 percent of the age seventy-five cohort have heart disease compared to the age eighteen to forty-four cohort, which have 4 percent.[14] There's about a ten-time differential. Hearing loss has about a three-time differential old and young. Diabetes is between four-six. We believe that workplace disability discrimination is an older worker issue.

What are some examples between the overlap of age and disability? There was a heart disease case in 2004 against a knife company.[15] The boss saw a subordinate's huge heart surgery scar, decided this was someone to move toward retirement, and the employee was fired. We got that turned around and summary judgment reversed. Another example is a case that involved the New York City police department. After decades of veteran police officers using hearing aids, suddenly all those officers were deemed no longer qualified to do the job. Hearing loss is one of those areas where workers between fifty and sixty-five have hearing issues but are incredibly reluctant to use assistive technology because it marks them as something that is the subject of employment discrimination. In another case,[16] a worker had sleep apnea and a heart rhythm disorder, and his employer told him he would have to leave because his health was bad, and he was getting older. The fact was that his performance was just fine. Summary judgment for the employer was reversed.

It is increasingly apparent that many of the issues traditionally associated with aging under the law–in transportation, housing, employments, community services–are appropriately also considered as disability discrimination issues. Gradually, the judicial system is recognizing the congruence of the two.

---

[14] Health, United States, 2010 available at http://www.cdc.gov/nchs/data/hus/hus10.pdf. *See* Table 49 at 208.

[15] *Adams v. Master Carvers of Jamestown, Ltd.*, 91 Fed. Appx. 718 (2nd Cir. 2004).

[16] *Flannery v. Recording Indus. Ass'n of Am.*, 354 F.3d 632 (7th Cir. 2004).

Offenders with Complex Communication Needs

Beverly L. Frantz, PhD[1]

> "Injustice anywhere is a threat to justice everywhere."
> Martin Luther King, Jr.

The purpose of this paper is to create awareness within the legal system of two emerging issues that significantly impact the lives of individuals with disabilities when they come into contact with the criminal justice system as victims, suspects, or offenders. The first issue involves individuals with complex communication needs. The second issue concerns the arrest of young, adult males with autism who are charged with possession and/or distribution of child pornography.

While little is known about the experiences of people with disabilities when they encounter the criminal justice system as victims, suspects, or offenders, copious studies have been conducted on the victimization of individuals with intellectual/developmental disabilities. Research indicates that persons with disabilities (40 percent) are more likely than people without disabilities (31 percent) to be attacked by persons known to them or who were casual acquaintances to them.[2] In 2014, the Center for Disease Control reported that people with intellectual and developmental disabilities, including autism, are "highly likely to be victims of all manner of criminal activity–from bullying to robbery to sexual assault." Sixty-seven percent of perpetrators who abuse

---

[1] Beverly L. Frantz is the criminal justice project director at Temple University's Institute on Disabilities Criminal Justice and Sexual Health Initiatives. She is faculty at AEquitas: The Prosecutors' Resource on Violence Against Women and at Temple University.

[2] Petersilia, J. (2001). *Crime Victims with Developmental Disabilities*. Washington DC: National Research Council/National Academy of Sciences.

individuals with severe cognitive disabilities access them through their work with disability services.[3]

Research also finds that people with intellectual disabilities comprise two to three percent of the general population, yet they comprise four to ten percent of the prison population, with even greater numbers in juvenile facilities and local jails.[4] In 2014, the Guide for Attorneys, New Jersey State Bar Foundation & the Criminal Justice Advocacy Program, Arc of New Jersey reported that an estimated thirty to forty percent of inmates in state prisons have an intellectual disability.[5] Once in the criminal justice system, people with disabilities are less likely to receive probation or parole, and more likely to serve a longer sentence because of their inability to understand or adapt to prison rules.

Crime against individuals with complex communication needs has received little research attention. A 2003 survey of forty adults with complex communication needs who used a variety of Augmentative and Alternative Communication modes found that 45 percent of individuals experienced crime or abuse.[6] Ninety-seven percent of those who experienced crime or abuse knew the perpetrators, 71 percent reported being victimized multiple times, and 66 percent experienced multiple types of victimization.[7] Only 28 percent reported their experiences to the police.[8] Long-term effects of the crimes included significant physical and emotional harm as well as loss of property or money.[9]

Communication, regardless of the mode, is essential in reporting neglect, abuse, sexual violence, and other criminal activity.

---

[3] Baladerian, N.J. (1991). *Sexual Abuse of People with Developmental Disabilities. Journal of Sexuality and Disability, (9) 4, 323-335.*

[4] Petersilia, J. (2000). *Invisible Victims: Violence Against Persons with Developmental Disabilities.* Human Rights. Chicago, Illinois: American Bar Association.

[5] Available at http://www.thearc.org/document.doc?id=4746.

[6] Bryen, N. D., Carney, A., Frantz, B. (2003). *Ending the Silence: Adults Who Use Augmentative Communication & Their Experiences as Victims of Crime.* Journal of Augmentative and Alternative Communication, 19 (2), 1twenty-five-134.

[7] *Id.*

[8] *Id.*

[9] *Id.*

People with complex communication needs are individuals who have significant difficulty being understood, especially by communication partners who are not familiar to them. Communication partners in the criminal justice system include, but are not limited to, police officers, detectives/investigators, attorneys, probation/parole officers, judges, and correctional officers. People with complex communication needs may also have problems understanding what others are saying. They may have other disabilities such as cerebral palsy, autism, and/or intellectual/developmental disabilities. They may use communication aids such as speech-generating devices or language/alphabet boards. They may need, but not have access to, such communications aids. It is important to remember that some people with complex communication needs may be able to read and spell.

All people communicate in some manner. Regardless of the extent or severity of a person's disability, a person has the right to: express personal preferences or feelings; reject or refuse undesired objects and/or events; have access at all times to any needed augmentative and alternative communication devices and other assistive devices; have those devices in good working order; and be communicated with in ways that are meaningful, understandable, and culturally and linguistically appropriate.

Approximately two million people in the United States have complex communication needs. This means eight to twelve Americans out of one thousand have significant difficulties communicating their needs. It has been suggested that the "best" victim is the one who cannot tell. The following two examples illustrate the unique issues victims with complex communication needs face when they encounter the criminal justice system.

In the first example, a young woman in her mid-twenties with complex communication needs reported to police she had been sexually assaulted by "Joey." The investigating officers had a difficult time understanding the young woman and included in their report that "Joey" was the alleged offender. The Office of the District Attorney agreed to move the case forward if the DNA confirmed the victim's identification. The DNA results eliminated "Joey," but showed a genetic connection to a member of Joey's extended family, named "Joe." As a result, the Office of the District Attorney dropped the charges against Joey and refused to charge Joe.

Did the victim misidentify her assailant, or did the police unintentionally record the wrong name? Did the victim say "Joe," but due to her complex communication needs the police mistakenly heard "Joey?"

This case was not prosecuted, and the victim continues to live with her extended family, which includes her assailant Joe.

The importance of active listening and accurately recording a victim's statement cannot be underestimated. It is extremely difficult for an individual with complex communication needs to report criminal activity, and equally as difficult when they do report, to have their cases prosecuted.

The second example pertains to a sixteen-year-old girl with multiple sclerosis and complex communication needs who used both her voice and her augmentative and alternative device to disclose to a teacher that her mother's boyfriend had "done" something to her.

The teacher notified the principal, who in turn contacted the police. The responding officers attempted to take her statement but had a difficult time understanding her. However, due to the willingness and support of one of the police officers and the district attorney's office to reach out to speech/language experts, the facts of the assault became clear, and the case was listed for trial.

Motions were made and argued by the defense regarding the victim's competency. The defense tried unsuccessfully to argue that the victim's inability to communicate in a "typical" manner indicated she was incompetent. A second defense argument addressed the issue of her AAC device. First, were the symbols/icons on the device placed on the device before or after the date of the alleged assault? Second, why was she not going to use the device in court?

In response, the victim's speech therapist assured the court that no new symbols/icons had been installed on her device since the initial allegations were made. As to the second question, over the three years it took for the case to go to trial, the victim's cerebral palsy had weakened her muscle strength and control, essentially limiting her ability to use her device for more than a few minutes at a time.

During the victim's testimony, the Judge allowed a "revoicer" to repeat every word and utterance made by the victim. The Judge allowed the revoicer as an accommodation under the Americans with Disabilities Act (ADA). The revoicer was considered a speech-language expert witness, who had extensive experience working with individuals with complex communication needs.

The purpose of a revoicer is to ensure that victims with complex communication needs have their voices heard in court. The revoicer stands behind the right shoulder of the victim and repeats every word and utterance made by the victim. If the revoicer cannot understand something the victim has said, the revoicer states, "Please repeat, the revoicer did not understand."

Part of the Voice Protocol requires that the revoicer meet with the victim as often as necessary to be comfortable with the victim's mode of communication. Nothing about the case or anything that could remotely be construed by the defense as suggestive or leading the victim is discussed with the revoicer.

At one point during this weeklong trial, a disability advocate and a detective were in the anteroom before going into court. Neither individual knew the other person or their role in the case. The detective expressed concern that there was yet another delay. He held up a folded sheet of paper with several sentences written on it. He made a comment about all the time that was being wasted on this case because he only had a few notes, adding "Well, if you can't understand them, then you don't have anything to write." Although he was a detective, he was called as a defense witness.

In this case, the defendant was convicted and sentenced to nine to twelve years in prison, and his appeals were denied.

Whether in the status of a victim, suspect, or defendant, individuals with complex communication needs face serious hurdles when encountering the criminal justice system.

Two individuals, one a victim and one a suspect, with very similar characteristics—each will receive decidedly different experiences in terms of communication when encountering the criminal justice system.

Victims seldom have their cases investigated, and when they are investigated few cases ever get to court. However, when the person is a suspect, the process is the opposite. Because of the difficulty with speech and language, cases seem fast tracked from arrest to jail. Suspects often unintentionally, due to cognition issues, waive their rights. The criminal justice system does not understand their communication mode, and individuals do not understand their legal rights.

The second emerging issue involves young men with high functioning autism who are arrested and charged with possession and/or distribution of Internet child pornography.

Over the past several years, many families and professionals have sought assistance from the Institute on Disabilities at Temple University in situations involving young men with high functioning autism arrested on child pornography charges. These situations all involved males between the ages of seventeen and twenty-six, who lived with their parents. All were high school graduates, one attended community college, were extremely computer literate, and all were arrested by federal authorities. In each situation, the young men admitted to watching child pornography, stated they received the images through file-to-file peer sharing, but that they did not search or request the images on their own.

The Institute on Disabilities does not provide clinical treatment or legal advice. Rather, the Criminal Justice Project at the Institute provides support and technical assistance to victims, suspects, or defendants with intellectual and developmental disabilities and their families when they encounter the criminal justice system.

For people with intellectual and developmental disabilities understanding how the criminal justice system works, whether as a victim or a suspect/defendant, is daunting. For anyone not familiar with criminal justice system, the lexicon and pace of the system can be unnerving and confusing.

These issues may be heightened for individuals with autism considering their unique attributes, such as minimal empathy, naiveté, inappropriate one-sided social interactions, pedantic and repetitious speech, and intense preoccupation with a circumscribed topic.[10]

One situation involved a young man with autism who was attending community college, living with his parents, and successfully working a part-time job in his community. As with many people with autism, he also had significant social deficits, no friends, was highly computer literate and communicated with others through file-to–file peer sharing.

While he was at community college, seven U.S Immigration and Customs Enforcement (ICE) agents came to his home, presented his mother with a search warrant, asked where his bedroom was, went right to his bedroom, and took his computer and all of his other electronic equipment and gadgets. As the agents were leaving, the lead agent suggested to the mother: "You know, ma'am, if I were you, I would call an attorney right away." The family took the agent's advice and hired a criminal defense attorney.

When he was eighteen years old and a high school graduate, this young man had asked his parents to remove the parental blocks that they had placed on his computer. Recognizing that he was going to community college in the fall and that he had always used his computer in an appropriate manner, they agreed to remove the parental blocks.

Hiring a criminal defense attorney who has relevant experience working with individuals with autism and with child pornography issues is difficult. As these parents discovered, attorneys were more comfortable communicating with them versus their son, the actual client.

This young man was charged with multiple criminal offenses, including possession and distribution of child pornography. When the case finally went to trial, he was charged with only one count of possession of child pornography. At sentencing, which finally occurred according to his mother, three years, two months, and twenty-nine days after the initial contact with U.S. Immigration and Customs Enforcement (ICE), the judge sentenced the young man to nine months

---

[10] Wing, L. (1981). *Asperger's Syndrome: A Clinical Account.* Psychological Medicine, *11*(1), 115-129.

of house arrest, five years of probation, and he was not required to register on any sex offender database.

Not being required to register as a sex offender is extremely important, as had he been required to register, he probably would have lost state and federal employment and housing assistance. He is required to wear an ankle bracelet but is permitted with adequate notice to move around the community. He is also permitted to use social media, but on a monitored computer.

In this case, the Institute on Disabilities provided current research articles and talking points about autism to the defense attorney, who shared this information with the prosecution and the judge. At sentencing, the judge commented on the record that the "articles were very instructional."

The larger questions raised by this type of case are: 1) is the intent of watching child pornography for sexual gratification; 2) how does a person's intense preoccupation with a circumscribed topic affect his ability to disengage from watching; 3) what role does naïveté and a limited capacity to form age appropriate relations play; and 4) what exactly is the person watching?

If we want to reduce the risk of individuals with autism watching child pornography, professionals outside of the criminal justice system need to have an idea of what is being watched. This is not to suggest that anyone other than criminal justice professionals should have access to and watch this material. Rather, the idea of understanding in general terms what is being viewed is helpful in developing risk reduction training programs and including the consequences for watching this type of material in sex education programs.

In the Canadian legal system, there are five tiers or levels of crimes regarding child pornography. These tiers range from just viewing images of children, to viewing images of children in suggestive positions, to viewing acts with other children, adults, and bestiality. We want to know at what level the person with autism is watching.

There was another wrinkle in what happened with this family. Mom and dad went on a Caribbean vacation with friends. On their return, the father was stopped by security, and all of his electronic devices were confiscated. He was informed that he could wait while security went through his electronics and possibly miss his flight, or he could make his flight, and security would mail him his equipment after it had been searched.

The father was flagged because his name was the authorized name on the Internet account used by his son and the rest of his family. This father was shocked. No one had informed the family that this would happen. Neither the ICE officers nor their son's attorney advised them that this is standard procedure. It is only through the families experiencing these situations that we are learning about these situations.

There has been a good deal of attention in recent years to violence against individuals with intellectual and developmental disabilities. However, there is limited research on people with complex communication needs and individuals with autism charged with child pornography offenses. To ensure equal justice for all, the criminal justice system and disability organizations/advocates must work together to ensure that The Americans with Disabilities Act (ADA) is understood and applied in the broadest sense in terms of reasonable accommodations within the criminal justice system.

Criminal Justice and Disability, a National Model

Leigh Ann Davis[1]

The Arc's National Center on Criminal Justice and Disability (NCCJD) is a training and technical assistance center funded by the Bureau of Justice Assistance (BJA) whose focus is on people with intellectual and developmental disabilities (I/DD) who get involved in the criminal justice system as either suspects/offenders or victims.[2] It was the passage of the ADA that originally brought me to this work and to The Arc at the age of twenty-four when The Arc received a grant through the Department of Justice to create materials for police officers, attorneys, and people with disabilities about how to communicate with each other. The project was created to support voluntary compliance of Title II of the ADA and focused on explaining different accommodations both the law enforcement and legal communities could use to ensure the rights of people with disabilities were protected and that they had equal access to obtaining justice within the criminal justice system.

One thing I'd like to point out is that even though NCCJD has a particular expertise and focus on I/DD because the Center is housed within The Arc, we see the creation of this Center as an opportunity to have cross-disability impact when it comes to criminal justice issues.

---

[1] Leigh Ann Davis, M.S.S.W., M.P.A., is program manager for The Arc's National Center on Criminal Justice and Disability.

[2] Information about NCCJD available online: http://www.thearc.org/NCCJD. The Arc is the largest community-based organization advocating for and with people with intellectual and developmental disabilities and their families. The Arc has long recognized and responded to the need for law enforcement training on people with these disabilities. In 1996, The Arc testified to the U.S. Commission on Civil Rights regarding law enforcement use of Title II accommodations. A number of The Arc's 650 chapters provide criminal justice related training, support or services at both local and state levels.

NCCJD has a national advisory committee that includes people and organizations that cut across various disability fields, such as Autism Spectrum Disorder, Down syndrome, and Fetal Alcohol Spectrum Disorder or FASD. We also work with a number of law enforcement agencies, such as the International Association of Chiefs of Police, the Police Executive Research Forum, the Police Foundation, and the National Sheriffs Association. The advisory committee also includes representation from the legal community, including the American Bar Association and the National Disability Rights Network. Early on in creating the Center, we felt it was imperative to try to get as many partners to the table as possible to start looking at the issues around criminal justice and disability in a holistic manner. Sharing expertise across fields is critical in effectively addressing these issues head-on and finding workable solutions. I'll discuss more about the products and services NCCJD offers as a way to begin providing practical solutions for criminal justice professionals, as well as self-advocates and their families.

There have been plenty of stories in the media that draw attention to law enforcement's questionable use of force involving minority populations in the criminal justice system. The shooting of an eighteen-year-old black man in August of 2014 that took place in Ferguson, Missouri, received national attention and resulted in angry protests by the community, sparking a national debate about police use of force.[3] In the case of Sheehan vs. the City of San Francisco,[4] police officers forcibly entered the room of Teresa Sheehan, knowing that she had mental illness, and shot her five times with no attempt to accommodate her disability by using de-escalation techniques that are commonly used on people with mental illness. The officers then requested immunity from a lawsuit claiming there was no established law requiring them to accommodate her mental illness. Inside the courtroom, Justice Sotomayor seemed to be the one voice of reason when she said, "Isn't the ADA intended to ensure that police officers try mitigation in these

---

[3] Available online: http://www.nytimes.com/interactive/2014/08/13/us/ferguson-missouri-town-under-siege-after-police-shooting.html?_r=0

[4] *City and County of San Francisco et al vs. Sheehan*, 575 U.S. (2015). Available online: http://www.supremecourt.gov/opinions/14pdf/13-1412_0pl1.pdf

situations before they jump to violence?" [5] NCCJD agrees that this is exactly why we have the ADA and why we are developing training for law enforcement that addresses use of force within this population of people with disabilities specifically.

The idea for a national center on criminal justice and disability was born around 1995, shortly after The Arc received funding for the first time to provide information about the ADA to professionals in the criminal justice system. That initial project opened our eyes to how much injustice this population was facing, and in so many facets of the system, and how little resources were available to address these problems.

However, there were others who planted the seed even before the ADA could provide relief. Delores Norley, a parent and active member of her local of The Arc in Florida, created the first four-page "training key" for law enforcement on people with I/DD, which eventually was reproduced and made available to law enforcement nationally by the International Association of Chiefs of Police. Because of her tireless advocacy work, she was able to get her state to provide mandatory training for law enforcement on this issue, and her training key laid the foundation for The Arc to develop a full curriculum for our roughly 700 network in 1998.[6]

Since that time, The Arc struggled to find funding to support projects on suspect/offender issues but has been able to obtain grants related to *victims* with disabilities though the Office for Victims of Crime (OVC). What's really exciting about our current grant to develop a national center is that we're able to look not only at suspect/offender issues, but victim issues as well. It is rare to be able to do both, given how funding streams are set up, and it provides us with a new opportunity to look at the full gamut of issues that people with disabilities are facing in the system, whether they're victimized or a suspect/offender.

---

[5] Available online at http://www.slate.com/articles/news_and_politics/ jurisprudence/2015/03/san_francisco_v_sheehan_supreme_court_case_police_ shot_mentally_ill_woman.html

[6] The Arc's history of criminal justice initiatives is available on-line: http://www. thearc.org/NCCJD/timeline

While research is lacking in this field, we know that this is a population that is over represented in the criminal justice system. The research we do have indicates that individuals with disabilities represent 4-10 percent of the prison population with even more in juvenile justice facilities and jails.[7] Also, a national survey of education services in juvenile corrections found that 33 percent received special education.[8] An estimated 70 percent of justice-involved youth have disabilities, which include psychiatric disabilities as well as I/DDs.[9] The funding for research in this area is sorely lacking, and NCCJD continues to advocate for funding to focus on answering some critical questions, such as identifying exactly how many people in our nation's jails and prisons have disabilities. We are developing strategic alliances within the criminal justice field to help answer these questions, and, as one example, spoke at the American Jail Association to raise awareness of the need for effective screening for these types of disabilities.

As a national center that provides information and referral and technical assistance, we are providing information every day on a broad range of issues as we try to provide help and educate both families and professionals about these issues. Education is critical because most criminal justice professionals don't realize or can't really appreciate exactly what makes a person with disabilities more vulnerable in the system.

For example, as suspects, people with I/DD often don't want their disability to be noticed and will try to hide it, making it hard for an officer to identify the disability. Many times people know that they could be taken advantage of or be looked down upon for having a disability, so they are afraid to disclose this about themselves. They

---

[7]   Petersilia, J. (August 2000). Doing justice? Criminal offenders with developmental disabilities. CPRC Brief, 12 (4), California Policy Research Center, University of California.

[8]   Quinn, et al (2005). Youth with disabilities in juvenile corrections: A national survey. Council for Exceptional Children, Vol. 71 (3). Available online: http://helpinggangyouth.homestead.com/disability-best_corrections_survey.pdf.

[9]   *Orphanages, training schools, reform schools and now this? Recommendations to prevent the disproportionate place and inadequate treatment of children with disabilities in the juvenile justice system* (June 2015). National Disability Rights Network, Washington, DC.

often pretend to understand their rights even though they do not, which is a particularly important issue when it comes to being read their Miranda rights. They often say what they think others want to hear, which makes it very easy to get a false confession. They typically have little options for alternative sentencing once they're in the system due to the lack of programs/resources available to this population within the community. They're often denied due process and effective representation. Once incarcerated, they are abused, exploited, and often excluded from rehabilitation programs.[10]

I also think it is important to include victims in this discussion, because the fact is, most of the time people with disabilities are going to experience both sides of this issue–being a suspect and a victim–within their lifetime. However, they are more likely to experience being a victim than a suspect. Perhaps not surprisingly, over the past fifteen years or so, more attention and federal support has been given to crime victims with disabilities than to suspects or defendants. Thanks to legislation advocating the addition of a question about disability to the existing National Crime Victim Survey[11], we now know just how often victimization is occurring among people with various types of disabilities, and the rate is very high. Based on survey data, people with disabilities are twice as likely to be victims of violent crimes when compared to those without disabilities. Violent crimes include rape, sexual assault, robbery, and aggravated or simple assault. When looking at the rate of victimization among people with different types of disabilities, people with cognitive disabilities face the highest risk of victimization, which is a primary reason why we feel this issue needs to be addressed at NCCJD and within the disability community collectively.

---

[10] Pathways to Justice™: *A comprehensive training program for law enforcement, victim service providers and attorneys on intellectual, developmental and other disabilities* (in development). The Arc's National Center on Criminal Justice and Disability, Washington, DC.

[11] U.S. Department of Justice, Bureau of Justice Statistics. Crime against people with disabilities, 2009-2012 Statistical Tables. Available online: http://www.bjs.gov/index.cfm?ty=pbdetail&iid=4884.

We know that people with disabilities are perceived to be easy targets for victimization. They're less likely to report victimization because they have less knowledge about or access to the system to do so. They may not even realize that what is happening to them is a crime or that it's even abuse, because they don't typically get education and training on these issues. The same characteristics that create vulnerabilities as suspects also create serious threats to their safety as potential victims. They're easily influenced by and eager to please others. They may think the perpetrator is a friend. This is really due to the issue of people with disabilities desperately wanting to be accepted and needing a safe and supportive peer group in their lives, since these are things they don't often get. They are often more likely to do whatever is necessary to feel like they're keeping a friend, even if that so-called friend is victimizing them in some way.

Another big challenge for victims with I/DD is not being considered a credible witness. Although people with I/DD can make excellent witnesses when given the right accommodations, because of the extra effort and time it takes to work with them or the professional's lack of knowledge or comfort working with people with I/DD, they are deemed "not credible" without being given a fair shot to prove otherwise. Then there are other disadvantages once a victim enters the system. They're frequently devalued, ignored, and their cases are rarely prosecuted. They are routinely excluded in the criminal justice system due to stereotyped views about people with disabilities.

An important point that criminal justice professionals must realize is that many times these disabilities are hidden. Hidden disabilities can pose the most serious threat to the person with disabilities because without recognition, zero accommodations can be provided. With regard to people with intellectual and developmental disabilities, approximately 87-89 percent of all people that have this type of a disability function on the upper end of the spectrum. It's not going to be immediately recognized unless the officer or attorney starts asking specific questions that reveal how little a person understands. NCCJD believes there needs to be more training about identifying disabilities to improve a person's equal access to justice. It's important to make sure that people in the criminal justice system understand just how easily this disability can be missed and the ramifications it can have in the person's life. For example, NCCJD provided training to ATF agents last year about the issue of recognizing people with "mild" I/DD specifically because news reporters discovered agents were using people with I/DD, some with IQs in the 50's where the disability was fairly obvious, as informants–citing they had no idea a disability was present–and then arresting them for charges which the agents led the unwitting person to participate in.[12]

False confessions are common due to a desire to please the officer or the investigator.[13] We've seen many times where people with I/DD are placed in institutional settings in order to "regain competency," which is not a realistic expectation for someone with this type of disability, and they end up there for years. They are often unable to assist in their own defense, and their rights are waived unknowingly.

To address these issues, it became clear that we needed to develop a national center that could bring this broad range of issues together in one place. There is a quote I like, "There is nothing more powerful than an idea whose time has come." As advocates who have worked within the disability and criminal justice field for many years, we believe our time has come. Now is the time for us to be able to come together and make real change. All of us within different sectors of the disability and criminal justice fields can begin creating a safe place where the community of people with disabilities, justice professionals, family members, and other advocates can discuss the challenging realities of our day. We are so excited to have that opportunity with this national center to begin conversations that can start bridging the gaps. Regardless of whether we use different language, different terminology, or we have different viewpoints on things, if we can find a place to start talking about these issues in a transparent way, we believe we have a chance to make some inroads and lasting progress.

---

[12] NCCJD blog available online: http://blog.thearc.org/2013/12/13/arc-calls-department-justice-end-tactics-thoroughly-investigate-allegations-people-disabilities-exploited-sting-operations/.

[13] *Perske's List: False confessions from 75 persons with intellectual disabilities. Intellectual and Developmental Disabilities* Vol. 49, No. 5, pp. 468–479, October 2011. Available online: http://www.thearc.org/NCCJD/materials/perske-list.

As I mentioned, The Arc's National Center on Criminal Justice and Disability is a training and technical assistance center funded by the Bureau of Justice Assistance. It's the first national effort of its kind that addresses both victim/witness and suspect/offender issues. We're a national clearinghouse for information and training on people with disabilities in the criminal justice system.

Our goal is to build capacity of the criminal justice system to respond to gaps in existing services for people with disabilities, with a focus on intellectual and developmental disability.

We have specific strategies in place to build capacity, because we've seen that many times grants are very short-lived, and therefore, short-sighted, and we don't have an opportunity to gain momentum so that we can sustain training and advocacy efforts. One challenge is that there's really no nationally unified group of advocates or self-advocates able to take this on at the level it needs to be addressed. In response to that, first of all, we created the Center; but secondly, we created the Pathways to Justice[14] training that creates Disability Response Teams[15] to sustain the training throughout the country. People with disabilities are involved in the DRTs and will help lead the way. We'll be piloting the training throughout 2015.

We've learned from experience that creating a training product in and of itself is not going to make the kind of lasting impact that this issue requires. We need to make sure there is buy-in for the training, and in order to make that happen, we have to bring together all the different players and find out what motivates our target audiences to obtain training in the first place. Does the professional in the criminal justice system have a specific reason to want to be trained on this issue? Do they have a child with a disability? What is their desire around this

---

[14] Pathways to Justice™: *A comprehensive training program for law enforcement, victim service providers and attorneys on intellectual, developmental and other disabilities* (in development). The Arc's National Center on Criminal Justice and Disability, Washington, DC.

[15] Pathways to Justice: *Disability Response Teams – The key to implementing and sustaining NCCJD's Pathways to Justice training.* Available online: http://www.thearc.org/document.doc?id=5114.

issue, and how do we help them see how they can be part of the solution and become a true "champion for justice?"

This is true for legal professionals as well as the victim advocates. We have to make sure that from the beginning before the first day of training, we already have a committed group of people that want to see this happen in their state or community. Once those people are identified, a Disability Response Team is born. While we're thankful for the training for law enforcement on mental illness given through Crisis Intervention Training[16] (or CIT for short), most of the time the area of intellectual developmental disability is only touched on. For example, out of a forty-hour week training officers only receive maybe two hours dedicated to that topic. We're looking at ways to make sure that officers understand other disabilities like autism and mild intellectual disability, which many times they're not even recognizing.

In order to provide an overview of the kind of issues that we're addressing and NCCJD's mission, we developed the Pathways to Justice video.[17] What is really important is the stories behind the statistics and that one develops a deep understanding about how critical these issues are and that we work together to do SOMETHING about it, whether the person is a suspect or a victim.

The Center is a resource for support and information about these issues. We provide information and referral and technical assistance, and have logged roughly twenty-five0 inquiries to date since the center opened. Our I&R service provides help with anything from death penalty cases, to sex offender cases, to cases involving sexual assault victims. Any case where a family needs help, or attorneys want specific information on a type of diagnoses, or law enforcement agencies need tips on de-escalation, we are here to provide resources and support.

We also offer a popular webinar series, and all webinars are free and archived on our website. Webinars include both victims and suspect/

---

16 CIT description available on National Alliance for the Mentally Ill website: http://www2.nami.org/template.cfm?section=CIT2

17 Pathways to Justice video available online: https://www.youtube.com/watch?v=aZXe03aaWJ0.

offender issues. We will also be releasing a white paper on the topic the same day of the webinar.[18]

We have many publications as well. We've created diagnoses-specific fact sheets on autism spectrum disorder, FASD, and other specific diagnoses. We also have an online resource library and state-by-state map that allows people to find resources specific to their own state.

We are also working toward creating a database of expert witnesses who have expertise in I/DD, as well as legal experts with expertise in I/DD. Our goal is to build a comprehensive database so that when questions like this come up about who has expertise in these fields, we have people that we can refer others to—because right now there's really no such database. There is no existing resource that focuses specifically on victims and suspects/offenders with intellectual disability.

---

[18] *Violence, abuse and bullying affecting people with intellectual/developmental disabilities: A call to action for the criminal justice community* (2015). The Arc's National Center on Criminal Justice and Disability (NCCJD), Washington, DC. Available online: http://www.thearc.org/document.doc?id=5145. Webinar available online: http://www.thearc.org/NCCJD/training/webinars/ archive#violence-in-the-lives-of-PWD.

Criminal Justice Training

Kathryn Walker[1]

The National Center on Criminal Justice and Disability has been working to develop the Pathways to Justice training curriculum.[2] It is based off of the sequential intercept model from the mental illness world, and we have adapted it for intellectual and developmental disabilities. The Arc has almost 700 chapters across the country. The goal is that each will recruit a disability response team leader, and we can be a home base in Washington, DC, but each will really take ownership in their community.

We have disability response teams hosted by chapters across the top, and then those DRTs are split into two categories: criminal justice professionals and the disability community. Criminal justice professionals are law enforcement officers, victim services providers, and attorneys. On the disability community side, there are family advocates and disability advocates other than The Arc and self-advocates, which we think are very important to making our training effective. Our expertise is intellectual and developmental disability, but we are very open and excited to make this a cross-disability initiative.

The disability response teams will be recruited in a specific location, and they will attend a daylong training. We'll start with everyone in the same room together, all these professionals, self-advocates, other disability professionals, family members, etc. We're going to talk about disability with them. We're going to start with the social model talking about some stereotypes that people might not even know that they have and move forward to the medical model, because the reality is our

---

[1]   Kathryn Walker is a criminal justice fellow at The Arc's National Center on Criminal Justice and Disability.

[2]   http://www.thearc.org/NCCJD/training

criminal justice system still uses that model whether we like it or not. Then we'll have a break for lunch, and afterward we will move on to our specific criminal justice professionals. At this point, the attorneys will be in a separate group from the service providers and the law enforcement officers in order to focus on the nitty-gritty of how to do their job well. Then we all come back together at the end of the day to go through case studies in order to talk about and apply the things that were learned.

We hope to use this model to facilitate discussion among criminal justice professionals and disability advocates in order to start bridging some of those cracks in the system. We're hoping that at each stage we can talk to these professionals about the need to identify, accommodate, and support people with disabilities. We're hoping that those three actions will be right on the top of the list after professionals have had our training. In addition, we hope that people will start talking to one another across some of these intercepts so that the police officer that is primarily involved in first contact is talking to the defense attorney who is working with someone who is currently in jail.

One example of an information and referral call that we received from Illinois involved a young man named Jack who had intellectual and developmental disabilities. He was charged with felony assault right after moving to a new group home. He had an altercation with a new housemate, and a third housemate called the police. When the police arrived on the scene, Jack ended up striking a police officer. Jack had tried to leave the scene because that was one of the coping strategies that he had been taught to use when he felt stressed out, and the police officer was not pleased with that response and grabbed him by the hoodie from behind and threw him to the ground, which Jack did not take very well. He ended up being tased, and it was a very ugly scene. He was read his Miranda rights on the spot, which he promptly waived. Jack had no idea what happened and received no assistance.

For us that's an example of a failure and breakdown at first contact.

Then Jack was transported to jail where he spent twenty-four hours without support or access to his medication. The jail never notified Jack's parents. After his parents found out he was in jail, they called to try to inform the supervisor of Jack's needs. The response from jail staff was that Jack should tell them what kind of medication he needed and how to get in touch with the pharmacy, which Jack was not able to do. He sat in jail without anything that he needed.

Then he was assigned a public defender for bond court. Initially bond was set at $30,000, which Jack certainly couldn't pay nor could his family. This is where we actually have a positive outcome. The public defender and an advocate in Jack's family reached out to us. We got together a plan for them, a way to outline supports and services that he had in the community in a way that the court could see it, read it, acknowledge it, and understand that there was a safety plan in place and that Jack was going to come back for court. After the family and everyone spoke to the judge, and he felt comfortable that there was a plan in place, Jack's bond was reduced to $10,000.

While out on bond, Jack was evaluated by the state psychiatrist and was found incompetent to stand trial. At that point, the state attorney still didn't want to dismiss the charges. Jack had to go back to the same state evaluator for a second evaluation for his sanity at the time of the incident, and he was found not sane at the time of the incident. Now we have someone incompetent to proceed and found not sane at the time of the incident, and still they're moving forward with the charges.

Eventually, with this plan, we were able to get a successful outcome. In this case, the charges were dismissed. However, Jack and his whole family were in and out of court from March 2014 all the way through October. This was months of stress for the family and use of resources in the system over this charge resulting from an incident at a group home.

When the case was finally dismissed, the family felt Jack had been misunderstood from the beginning. They believed the court did not understand the difference between mental illness and developmental disability because the judge would speak to Jack as though he had a normal IQ but was experiencing mental illness. We see this systematically. There is not necessarily a clear job of distinguishing between intellectual and developmental disability and mental illness.

Here is a quote from Jack: "My heart was racing because I was in the back of a squad car handcuffed and then at the police station. I pretty much felt like a nervous wreck. I felt sick to my stomach because I was around people I didn't know. A couple days before court, I felt scared and nervous. I felt really scared that I was going to jail. The judge calmly talked to me and explained what would happen the next time I got in trouble, but I was still edgy. I feel more calmly now that it's over."[3] It was a traumatic experience for the whole family.

---

[3] The Arc, *Case Dismissed: National Center on Criminal Justice and Disability Provides Critical Support to Bring Justice in Illinois*, available at http://blog.thearc. org/2014/11/21/case-dismissed-national-center-criminal-justice-disability-provides-critical-support-bring-justice-illinois/ (Nov. 21, 2014).

Author Biographies

Editor

David Ferleger has a national law and consulting practice specializing in appeals and Supreme Court representation, public interest, civil rights, and disability law. He has litigated landmark disability cases, argued five times before the Supreme Court of the United States, and participated in other cases before the Court. He successfully represented individuals with mobility disabilities in opposing Supreme Court review of their victory in the landmark *Frame v. City of Arlington* case in 2012. He represents Disability Rights Advocates for Technology in the Supreme Court in a petition challenging Walt Disney World's ban on Segway use by people with disabilities. In addition, Mr. Ferleger currently serves a federal judge as "independent consultant and monitor" in a disabilities class action, and another federal judge as technical advisor for implementation of a settlement. He is a founding member of the Academy of Court Appointed Masters. Mr. Ferleger has taught at the New York University Law School and the University of Pennsylvania Law School. His writing in the disabilities field has included book chapters, books of legal materials, law review articles, and popular magazine and newspaper articles. He holds BA and JD degrees from the University of Pennsylvania.

Authors

Kelly Bagby is a senior attorney at AARP Foundation Litigation (AFL) and specializes in civil rights, disability rights, special education, health law, and other public interest areas, with an emphasis on litigation. She has been a part of AFL's Health Team since 2008. She has litigated a range of discrimination and public interest cases in federal and state courts. Recently, she has been counsel or co-counsel in class action lawsuits to seek restoration of cuts to Medi-Cal program funding, obtain assistance for nursing facility residents transitioning to the community, and to obtain relief for a class of California nursing facility residents who were administered psychotropic medications without informed consent. Prior to joining AFL, she worked for the Office of Counsel for the Office of Inspector General (OIG) for the United States Department of Health and Human Services from 2004 until 2008. Before 2004, she was the legal director for the District of Columbia's Protection and Advocacy Program, University Legal Services, and also worked for the Maryland Disability Law Center (MDLC). She is a member of the MDLC Board of Directors. Ms. Bagby is a graduate of Franklin and Marshall College and the University of Baltimore School of Law.

Peter Blanck is university professor at Syracuse University, the highest faculty rank, which has only been granted to eight other individuals in the history of the university. He also is chairman of the Burton Blatt Institute (BBI). Prior to joining the faculty at Syracuse, Professor Blanck was Kierscht professor of law and director of the Law, Health Policy, and Disability Center at the University of Iowa. Professor Blanck is honorary professor at the Centre for Disability Law & Policy at the National University of Ireland, Galway. He is chairman of the Global Universal Design Commission (GUDC), and president of Raising the Floor (RtF) USA. Prior to teaching, Professor Blanck practiced law at Covington & Burling, and served as law clerk to the late Honorable Carl McGowan of the United States Court of Appeals for the DC Circuit. Blanck holds a JD from Stanford University, where he was president of the *Stanford Law Review*; and a PhD in social psychology from Harvard University. Professor Blanck's most recent book is *e-Quality: The Struggle for Web Accessibility by People with Cognitive Disabilities* (2014).

Hon. Richard Brown is chief judge for the Wisconsin Court of Appeals. He was first elected as an appellate judge to the Court of Appeals for District 2 in 1978 and was appointed chief judge in 2007. Judge Brown is a member of the Wisconsin Law School Board of Visitors; the Council of Chief Judges of State Courts of Appeal, Administration of Justice Committee; and the ABA Commission on Lawyer Assistance Programs, chairing the Judicial Assistance Initiative, which promotes mental wellness for judges. He is also co-author and current revision editor for *Standards of Review in*

Wisconsin. In the past, Judge Brown has been chair of the Committee to Improve Interpreting and Translation in Wisconsin Courts, co-chair of the Individual Rights and Responsibilities Section of the ABA Committee on the Rights of Persons with Disabilities, and chair of the ABA Commission on Mental and Physical Disability Law. He was also a member of the Wisconsin Planning and Policy Advisory Committee and co-chair of the Efficiencies Subcommittee. Judge Brown has lectured on the Americans with Disabilities Act at judicial conferences throughout the United States. Prior to being elected to serve on the court, Judge Brown was an attorney in private practice from 1973 to 1978, and was assistant district attorney for Racine County from 1971 to 1973. He holds a BA from Miami University, a JD from the University of Wisconsin Law School, and an LLM from the University of Virginia.

Leigh Ann Davis is program manager for The Arc's National Center on Criminal Justice and Disability. With almost twenty years of experience in the intellectual and/or developmental disability (I/DD) and criminal justice field at the national level, Ms. Davis has worked with both disability and criminal justice professionals and agencies, as well as people with disabilities, to build stronger lines of open communication and understanding between these two worlds to ensure that people with I/DD have access to accommodations in the criminal justice system, whether suspect, offender, or victim. She has authored numerous publications, including curricula, scholarly articles, fact sheets, and other publications on a broad array of criminal justice topics (including victims, suspects/offenders, death penalty, victims with FASD) and presents at state, national, and international conferences to enlighten others about the unique issues faced by people with I/DD in the criminal justice system. As The Arc's subject matter expert related to criminal justice and disability issues, she is often interviewed by local and national media outlets regarding criminal justice and disability issues, and high profile cases (including an interview by Alyona Minkovski for "HuffPost Live" in December 2014). Ms. Davis also serves as a consultant for The Office for Victims of Crime (OVC) Training and Technical Assistance Center, and Vera Institute of Justice. She holds a BSW, MSSW, and MPA from the University of Texas at Arlington.

Robert Dinerstein is professor of law, associate dean for Experiential Education, and director of the Disability Rights Law Clinic at American University Washington College of Law, where he has taught since 1983. Prior to joining the faculty at American University, Professor Dinerstein was an attorney in the Special Litigation Section, Civil Rights Division, United States Department of Justice. He served on the President's Committee on Mental Retardation (now called the President's Committee on People with Intellectual Disabilities) from 1994 to 2001. He has consulted for the World Health Organization regarding the revision of mental health laws in Ghana and Malawi, and for the Open Society Foundations on various projects, including their support of disability rights clinics and curricula in Southern Africa and Latin America. Professor Dinerstein currently sits on the boards of the Quality Trust for Individuals with Disabilities, Inc. (president) and the Equal Rights Center (president), and in the past has served on the boards of a number of other public interest and disability rights organizations. He has made numerous presentations and published a number of articles, chapters, and other writings on disability law and clinical legal education, and is the co-author/co-editor, with Herr & O'Sullivan, of *A Guide to Consent* (AAMR 1999) and co-author of *Lawyers and Clients: Critical Issues in Interviewing and Counseling* (West Academic 2009). Professor Dinerstein is the 2013 winner of the Paul G. Hearne Award for Disability Rights from the ABA Commission on Disability Rights. He received his AB degree from Cornell University and his JD degree from Yale Law School.

Beverly Frantz is the project director for Temple University's Institute on Disabilities criminal justice and sexual health initiatives. She is faculty at AEquitas: The Prosecutors' Resource on Violence Against Women and at Temple University. Her focus is on the development and implementation of projects relating to sexual violence against individuals with disabilities; criminal justice issues, including communication access to the criminal justice system for victims and defendants; and sexuality training. Dr. Frantz is the author of peer reviewed journal articles, DVDs, book chapter, and personal safety/sexual abuse curricula for adults with intellectual and developmental disabilities. She earned a master of science degree from Villanova University and the London School of Economics, and a doctorate degree from Widener University in Human Sexuality.

Daniel F. Goldstein is a partner at the firm of Brown, Goldstein & Levy, LLP, and he has been a disability rights lawyer for more than two decades. As counsel for the National Federation of the Blind, Mr. Goldstein has initiated a national legal campaign to ensure access to technology used in the classroom, workplace, and in everyday life. He secured a consent decree against Atlantic Cape Community college and entered into settlement agreements with Penn State and Florida State Universities that produced commitments to make the electronic and information technology systems used at these institutions accessible to blind students and faculty. Mr. Goldstein filed litigation against Arizona State University and complaints against five other universities piloting the inaccessible Kindle DX eBook reader. His efforts led to agreements to use only accessible e-book reading technology in their respective educational programs. Other cases brought by Mr. Goldstein have helped to ensure the accessibility of ATMs, the right of the blind to vote privately and independently, and to use a laptop computer equipped with screen reading software in high-stakes testing. His suit against Target.com set precedent regarding the application of access laws to websites. In addition to litigation, he has also been involved in the negotiation of joint technology agreements with technology developers such as Apple to make iTunes and iTunes U accessible. Mr. Goldstein, with Jonathan Lazar and Anne Taylor, co-authored *Ensuring Digital Accessibility through Process and Policy*, a book on the best practices for implementing IT accessibility in the public and private sector. Mr. Goldstein is a graduate of the University of Texas School of Law, and he clerked for Judge Frank A. Kaufman on the United States District Court for the District of Maryland. Prior to joining Brown, Goldstein & Levy, he served as an assistant United States attorney.

Vanita Gupta is principal deputy assistant attorney general and acting assistant attorney general for the Civil Rights Division at the United States Department of Justice. Prior to joining the department, Ms. Gupta served as deputy legal director of the American Civil Liberties Union (ACLU), and director of its Center for Justice. Previously, she was an attorney for its Racial Justice Program. Over her career, Ms. Gupta has earned a reputation for working closely and collaboratively with law enforcement, departments of corrections, and across the political spectrum to advance smart policing and criminal justice reforms. Through her work with the ACLU, she has been involved in reform initiatives around the country pertaining to federal and state policing, sentencing, drug policy, and criminal law. Her recent work has focused on building a bipartisan consensus to end overreliance on incarceration. Ms. Gupta began her career as a lawyer with the NAACP Legal Defense and Educational Fund. In addition, she has taught civil rights litigation and advocacy clinics at New York University School of Law since 2008. Ms. Gupta received a BA, magna cum laude, from Yale University and a JD from New York University School of Law.

Daniel Kohrman is a senior attorney with AARP Foundation Litigation (AFL), a public interest legal advocacy unit housed in the AARP Foundation, AARP's 501(c)(3) affiliate. He focuses on trial and appellate litigation for older workers, mostly discrimination cases on grounds of disability and/or age, under federal and/or state law. Recently, Mr. Kohrman settled disability bias claims against CoachUSA, persuading the national bus company to refine its qualification standards for drivers with diabetes. He also has filed numerous appellate amicus briefs on behalf of AARP urging vigorous enforcement of the ADA—both before and after the ADA Amendments Act became law. Mr. Kohrman and his colleagues also have represented older workers terminated in reductions-in-force at Ford Motor Co., Goodyear Tire & Rubber, Sprint, and credit card issuer Capital One; and they have brought other major age bias claims against Allstate, Seagate Technologies, 3M, and health insurer Wellpoint. Before joining AFL in 2001, Mr. Kohrman worked for the Civil Rights Division of the U.S. Justice Department, the Lawyers Committee for Civil Rights Under Law, and the law firm of Hogan & Hartson, where he sued states to require them to contribute to desegregation of urban schools. He has served on the executive board of the National Employment Lawyers' Association (NELA) since 2007, and was a member of the American Diabetes Association's board of directors from 2010-13.

Dr. Marc Maurer, of Baltimore, Maryland, is the immediate past president of the National Federation of the Blind (NFB), the largest consumer organization of blind people in the United States. He was elected in 1986 and held the position until 2014. He currently holds the position of director of legal policy for the National Federation of the Blind.

Dr. Maurer graduated cum laude from the University of Notre Dame in 1974. He then enrolled at the University of Indiana, School of Law, where he received his doctor of jurisprudence in 1977. In 1981 he went into private practice in Baltimore, Maryland, where he specialized in civil litigation and property matters. Increasingly, he concentrated on representing blind individuals and groups in the courts. Today he is one of the most experienced and knowledgeable attorneys in the country regarding the laws, precedents, and administrative rulings concerning civil rights and discrimination against the blind. He is a member of the Bar in Indiana, Ohio, Iowa, and Maryland, and a member of the Bar of the Supreme Court of the United States.

Dr. Maurer received numerous awards and spoke in a multitude of influential forums throughout his twenty-eight-year presidency. He received the Heritage Award from the Canadian National Institute for the Blind and the United States Presidential Medal for Leadership in 1990, the *Baltimore Business Journal*'s 1999 Innovation Award, the VME Robert Dole Award in 2002, and the *Daily Record*'s 2002 Innovator of the Year award. Dr. Maurer joined President George W. Bush in the Oval Office in 2001 to celebrate the success of the NFB Everest Expedition and again for the signing of the Help America Vote Act of 2002. He received the Mayor's Business Recognition Award in 2007, the Rev. John J. Cavanaugh Award from the University of Notre Dame Alumni Association in 2009, and the Paul G. Hearne Award for Disability Rights from the American Bar Association in 2011.

He received honorary doctorate degrees from California's Menlo College in 1998, the University of Louisville in 1999, and from both the University of South Carolina Upstate and the University of Notre Dame in 2010.

Dr. Maurer delivered an address at the Kennedy School of Government at Harvard University in 1987. In 2009, he addressed the annual convention of Blind Citizens Australia at the University of Queensland. He delivered addresses on civil rights at Oxford University and Birmingham University in the United Kingdom during 2000. In 2013 he gave the keynote speech at the First International Conference on Technology for Helping People with Special Needs at the Al-Imam Mohammad Ibn Saud Islamic University in the Kingdom of Saudi Arabia.

Arlene B. Mayerson has been directing attorney of the Disability Rights Education and Defense Fund since 1981. She is a leading expert in disability rights law and a key advisor to Congress and the disability community on major disability rights legislation, including the Handicapped Children's Protection Act and the Americans with Disabilities Act (ADA). Ms. Mayerson provided expert testimony before several Congressional committees when they were debating the ADA, and she filed comments on the ADA regulations for more than five hundred disability rights organizations. She has provided representation, consultation to counsel, and coordination of amicus briefs on key disability rights cases before the U.S. Supreme Court. Ms. Mayerson was appointed by the Secretary of the U.S. Department of Education to the Civil Rights Reviewing Authority, responsible for reviewing the civil rights decisions of the department. Ms. Mayerson is a lecturer in disability law at the University of California, Berkeley and has published widely on disability rights and the ADA. She received her LLM from Georgetown University, JD from Boalt Hall, and BS from Boston University.

Ari Ne'eman is the president and co-founder of the Autistic Self Advocacy Network, an advocacy organization run by and for autistic adults seeking to increase the representation of autistic people across society. He is an autistic adult and a leading advocate in the neurodiversity and self-advocacy movements. Mr. Ne'eman was nominated by President Obama to the National Council on Disability and currently chairs the Council's Entitlements Committee, serving previously as the chair of the Policy & Program Evaluation Committee. In addition, Mr. Ne'eman serves as co-director of the LEAD Center's public policy team. He has worked on a variety of disability rights legislation relating to education, transition, employment, and rights protection. Mr. Ne'eman also served as a public member of the Interagency Autism Coordinating Committee, a federal advisory committee that coordinates with the Department of Health and Human Services concerning autism. He served at the state level in New Jersey as well. He is a board member of TASH, an advocacy organization focusing on advancing social justice for people with significant disabilities. Mr. Ne'eman received a BA from the University of Maryland-Baltimore County.

Julie Nepveu is a senior attorney at AARP Foundation Litigation (AFL), where she focuses on disability rights, consumer protection, affordable utilities, and fair housing. Ms. Nepveu litigates impact cases, files litigation and amicus briefs on issues affecting older persons in courts across the country, and drafts comments to federal regulatory proposals. Currently, she is representing plaintiffs in a class action challenging ADA paratransit violations against the Maryland Transit Administration. Prior to joining AFL, Ms. Nepveu worked as a staff attorney in the Housing and Community Development Project of the Lawyers' Committee for Civil Rights under Law and served as the legal director for the National Coalition for Disability Rights. She also represented tenants in landlord tenant and subsidized housing matters at Legal Services of Northern Virginia. Ms. Nepveu serves on the board of directors for the ENDependence Center of Northern Virginia. She served as a judicial law clerk to Judge Thomas Lydon at the U.S. Claims Court after receiving her JD from the University of Maine School of Law.

Laurence Paradis is executive director and co-director of litigation for Disability Rights Advocates (DRA). He has handled many precedent-setting ADA cases in areas such as employment, housing, transportation, education, insurance, and public accommodations. Prior to co-founding DRA, Mr. Paradis worked as an associate and partner at Miller, Starr, and Regalia. Currently, Mr. Paradis is a member of the Pregnancy Accommodation Working Group at WorkLife Law at UC Hastings. He is a past member of the President's Committee on the Employment of People with Disabilities, and has been on the boards of many advocacy organizations such as the Berkeley Center for Independent Living, National Council on Disability, International Watch Committee, American Civil Liberties Union of Northern California, and the Berkeley Commission on Disability. In addition, Mr. Paradis has assisted the courts as a court-appointed mediator, as a ninth circuit judicial council lawyer representative from the U.S. District Court for the Northern District of California, and as a member of a Magistrate Judge Selection Panel, U.S. District Court for the Northern District of California. Mr. Paradis is a graduate of Harvard Law School.

Elizabeth Pendo is vice dean and professor of law at Saint Louis University School of Law. She has a secondary appointment as professor of health management and policy at Saint Louis University School of Public Health, and is a member of the Center for Health Law Studies and the William C. Wefel Center for Employment Law at the School of Law. Professor Pendo is a nationally recognized expert in disability law and healthcare law. Her scholarship focuses on the difference disability makes in places in our society, such as the healthcare system and the workplace, with a particular interest in legal and social meanings of disability and their relationship to classifications based on gender, race, and genetic information. Other projects include civil rights and healthcare reform approaches to health disparities for people with disabilities; models of disability and their impact on healthcare; public right-of-way and accessibility issues in the city of Saint Louis; and genetic testing in the workplace and its intersections with classifications based on gender, race, class, and disability. Professor Pendo has published with a number of law journals and peer-reviewed journals across the country, including, *U.C. Davis Law Review, Utah Law Review, Yale Journal of Health Policy, Law and Ethics, Connecticut Insurance Law Journal, The Journal of Legal Medicine,* and *The Harvard Women's Law Journal.* She frequently submits testimony and comment to federal agencies and legislatures on issues relating to her work. In addition, she is an elected member of the American Law Institute.

Mark A. Riccobono is President of the National Federation of the Blind. Prior to becoming President, he served as executive director of the National Federation of the Blind Jernigan Institute where he was responsible for the development of many innovative national education and technology programs such as the National Center for Blind Youth in Science, Braille Enrichment for Literacy and Learning (BELL), and the Blind Driver Challenge. Prior to joining the National Federation of the Blind, Mr. Riccobono participated in the Sears executive training program, was appointed to the Wisconsin State Superintendent's Blind and Visual Impairment Education Council, and served as the first director of the Wisconsin Center for the Blind and Visually Impaired, an agency responsible for statewide services to blind children. In 2010-2011, he served as an appointed member of the Federal Commission on Accessible Instructional Materials in Postsecondary Education. Mr. Riccobono earned an undergraduate degree in business administration from the University of Wisconsin-Madison, and a graduate degree in educational studies from the Johns Hopkins University.

Howard Rosenblum is chief executive officer of the National Association of the Deaf (NAD), the largest and most influential membership organization of deaf and hard of hearing persons in the United States. He also is the legal director of the NAD Law and Advocacy Center and oversees its legal staff. Prior to joining the NAD in 2011, he handled disability rights litigation for nineteen years: nine years at Equip for Equality and ten years with a private firm. In 1997, he founded the Midwest Center on Law and the Deaf (MCLD) to address the lack of access to the legal profession for deaf and hard of hearing individuals and oversaw its operation as the board chair until 2011. He is the primary author of the American Bar Association *Guidelines on Court Access for Deaf and Hard of Hearing People* and the sixth edition of the NAD *Legal Rights: Guide for Deaf and Hard of Hearing People*. President Barack Obama appointed Mr. Rosenblum to serve on the United States Access Board in 2010 and reappointed him in 2014. He holds an undergraduate computer engineering degree from the University of Arizona and a JD from Chicago-Kent College of Law.

Fredric K. Schroeder is a research professor with the San Diego State University Research Foundation. He works in the area of vocational rehabilitation policy and leadership. He is also the executive director of the National Rehabilitation Association and first vice president of the World Blind Union. Prior to joining the faculty at San Diego State University, Professor Schroeder served as the ninth commissioner of the Rehabilitation Services Administration (RSA). President Clinton appointed him to this position in 1994. In the mid-1980s, he was appointed to be the first executive director of the New Mexico Commission for the Blind. When he left in 1994, the commission held the record for placing consumers into jobs with the highest hourly earnings for blind people anywhere in the nation. Professor Schroeder was also a pioneer in the field of orientation and mobility. He was the first blind person in the nation to be admitted to a university program in orientation and mobility; he blazed the trail that led to the certification of blind orientation and mobility instructors. He is an accomplished scholar with over fifty published articles and a nationally and internationally recognized lecturer on disability policy. Professor

Schroeder holds a BA and MA from San Francisco State University, and a PhD in education administration and leadership from the University of New Mexico.

Anita Silvers is chair of the San Francisco State University Philosophy Department. She has published many articles and book chapters, and several books, including *Disability, Difference, Discrimination: Perspectives on Justice in Bioethics and Public Policy* (recently reissued in a new edition), *Americans with Disabilities* (with Leslie Francis), and *Medicine and Social Justice: Essays on the Distribution of Health Care* (with Rosamond Rhodes and Margaret Battin). She is the recipient of the Phi Beta Kappa/APA Lebowitz Prize for Excellence in Philosophical Thinking, the APA Quinn Prize for Service to Philosophy and Philosophers, and the California Faculty Association Human Rights Award. Ms. Silvers served on the National Council for the Humanities, appointed by the President of the United States. She is a longtime (fifty years) activist for disability and civil rights.

Susan Ann Silverstein is a senior attorney for AARP Foundation Litigation where she works on fair housing, disability rights, and low-income issues. Ms. Silverstein has litigated significant cases establishing the rights of people with disabilities in public and private housing, including assisted living, retirement communities, and in the context of community planning and redevelopment. This year will mark the twenty-fifth anniversary of the decision she received in *Cason v. Rochester Housing Authority,* the first case brought on behalf of renters with disabilities under the 1988 Fair Housing Amendments Act that established that housing providers could not determine whether applicants were capable of living independently but could only screen for their ability to meet relevant lease requirements. Ms. Silverstein received her BS from the Massachusetts Institute of Technology and her JD from Columbia University School of Law. She was a Community Builder Fellow with the Department of Housing and Urban Development in conjunction with the Harvard Kennedy School of Government. She began her career as a Reginald Heber Smith Fellow at Southern Tier Legal Services in Bath, NY, and worked for other legal services offices in Western New York.

Christopher Slobogin occupies the Milton R. Underwood Chair in Law at the Vanderbilt Law School, where he directs the Criminal Justice Program. Professor Slobogin also holds a secondary appointment as an affiliate professor of psychiatry in the Vanderbilt School of Medicine. He has authored scores of articles on criminal procedure, and his book *Psychological Evaluations for the Courts* (3rd edition, 2007), which he co-authored with another lawyer and two psychologists, is considered the standard-bearer in forensic mental health. According to the *Leiter Report*, he is one of the five most cited criminal law and procedure law professors in the nation. Before joining Vanderbilt's law faculty in 2008, Professor Slobogin held the Stephen C. O'Connell Chair at the University of Florida's Levin College of Law, and also taught at Stanford, the University of Southern California, and the University of Virginia Law Schools. He has appeared on *Good Morning America*, *Nightline*, the *Today Show*, *National Public Radio*, and many other media outlets, and has been cited in more than two thousand law review articles or treatises and more than one hundred judicial opinions, including at the Supreme Court level. Professor Slobogin is an honorary distinguished member of the American Psychology-Law Society, and he has served as chair of the American Bar Association's task force to revise the Criminal Justice Mental Health Standards, as well as reporter for the ABA's task forces on the insanity defense and on mental disability and the death penalty. He holds an AB from Princeton University, and a JD and LLM from the University of Virginia.

Kathryn Walker is a criminal justice fellow at The Arc's National Center on Criminal Justice and Disability. While completing her graduate course work at the University of Miami, Ms. Walker worked in the Health Rights Clinic, a medical legal partnership handling veteran's benefits, social security disability, and permanency planning. She also worked on the Institutional Conditions team at Disability Rights Florida, and interned with Department of Justice, Civil Rights, Disability Rights Section in Washington, DC. Ms. Walker was an articles and comments editor on the Inter-American Law Review, and also a Miami Scholar and HOPE Fellow—both scholarship programs based on commitment to public service. Before joining The Arc in December 2013, she completed her MPH as a legal policy intern for the Judge David L. Bazelon Center for Mental Health Law. Prior to attending law school, she worked for Residential Services, Inc. in Chapel

Hill, North Carolina, while receiving her BA from the University of North Carolina at Chapel Hill. Ms. Walker received her JD and MPH from the University of Miami.

Michael Waterstone is visiting professor of law at Northwestern Law School for the 2014-2015 academic year. He is also associate dean for research and academic centers and the J. Howard Ziemann Fellow and professor of law at Loyola Law School. Prior to joining the Loyola faculty, Professor Waterstone taught at the University of Mississippi Law School and worked as an associate in the Los Angeles law firm of Munger, Tolles & Olson. He also clerked for the Honorable Richard S. Arnold on the United States Court of Appeals for the Eighth Circuit. Professor Waterstone is one of the co-authors of a leading casebook on disability law, and his articles have appeared in journals such as *Harvard Law Review, Notre Dame Law Review, Minnesota Law Review, Duke Law Journal, Vanderbilt Law Review*, and *Northwestern Law Review*. He advises and consults with several policy organizations on national and international disability issues, including the Harvard Law School Project on Disability, Human European Consultancy, the Burton Blatt Institute, the Disability Rights Legal Center, the World Bank, and the National Council on Disability. Professor Waterstone has testified before the United States Senate on issues relating to veterans with disabilities and older voters. He is a member of the California State Bar's Commission on Access and Fairness, the former chair of the American Association of Law Schools' Section on Disability Law, and a former board member of the Disability Rights Legal Center. Professor Waterstone is a former commissioner on the American Bar Association's Commission on Disability Rights. He holds a BA from the University of California, Los Angeles, and a JD from Harvard Law School.

www.ingramcontent.com/pod-product-compliance
Lightning Source LLC
Chambersburg PA
CBHW031050180526
45163CB00002BA/764